TRANSFORMATION

"Thorough in detail. It's hard to walk away from this book without an altered perspective on human life!"
—*South Bend Tribune*

"Strieber is convincing."
—*Rocky Mountain News*

BREAKTHROUGH

". . . Strieber's purported proof of alien vistors will at least give you serious pause."
—*Kirkus Reviews*

THE SECRET SCHOOL

"*The Secret School* is Whitley Strieber's courageous journey to childhood in search of truth. Do not settle your own accounts with reality until you read this."

—Larry Dossey, M.D.
Author of *Prayer Is Good Medicine*
and *Healing Words*

"Whitley Strieber delves into the magic of a childhood punctuated with vertiginous terrors and gently brushed with the wings of cherubs. What he brings back for us is . . . a message of hope that we cannot afford to ignore."

—Dr. Jacques Vallée
Author of *Dimensions,*
Passport to Magonia,
and *Messengers of Deception*

The
SECRET SCHOOL

PREPARATION FOR CONTACT

Whitley Strieber

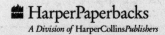

📚 HarperPaperbacks
A Division of HarperCollins*Publishers*

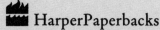

HarperPaperbacks

A Division of HarperCollins*Publishers*
10 East 53rd Street, New York, N.Y. 10022-5299

Copyright © 1997 by Walker & Collier, Inc.
All rights reserved. No part of this book may be used or
reproduced in any manner whatsoever without written
permission of the publisher, except in the case of brief
quotations embodied in critical articles and reviews.
For information address HarperCollins*Publishers,*
10 East 53rd Street, New York, N.Y. 10022-5299.

A hardcover edition of this book was published in 1997 by
HarperCollins*Publishers.*

ISBN 0-06-109618-0

HarperCollins®, 🔥®, and HarperPaperbacks™
are trademarks of HarperCollins*Publishers* Inc.

Cover Design by Carl Galian

Cover illustration © 1997 by Lee MacLeod

First HarperPaperbacks printing: December 1997

Printed in the United States of America

Visit HarperPaperbacks on the World Wide Web at
http://www.harpercollins.com

❖ 10 9 8 7 6 5 4 3 2 1

This book is dedicated to the memory of
ALINE CARTER,
poet laureate of Texas, visionary, guide to the stars.

ACKNOWLEDGMENTS

I would like to thank Ed Conroy and Anne Strieber for their efforts on behalf of this book, David Carter for allowing me access to his mother's home, Lanette Glasscock, Charles Cockerell, and all the others who so kindly contributed to the investigation of strange phenomena in the Olmos Basin in San Antonio.

TIME

Time is the root of all this earth;
These creatures, who from Time had birth,
Within his bosom at the end
Shall sleep; Time hath no enemy nor friend.

All we in one long caravan
Are journeying since the world began;
We know not whither, but we know
Time guideth at the front, and all must go.

—BHARTRHARI
translated by Paul E. More
from the Sanskrit

CONTENTS

··

Acknowledgments   vii
The Discovery   xiii

FIRST TRIAD   A Child Awakes   1

Lesson 1: The Coming of the
       Sisters of Mercy   3
Lesson 2: The Angel of the Jails   19
Lesson 3: The Man in the
       Lightning   35

SECOND TRIAD   The Telescope   59

Lesson 4: Eddie Death   61
Lesson 5: The Wall of Fear   75
Lesson 6: The Secret of the Comets   97

CONTENTS

THIRD TRIAD The School 129

Lesson 7: Time Traveler 131
Lesson 8: The Human Past 157
Lesson 9: The Future 191

Secret No More 223

Lesson 10: A New Lesson 225

Final Commentary: The Path to Joy 241

From the Author 253

Afterword by Ed Conroy 257

The
SECRET SCHOOL

PREPARATION FOR CONTACT

WE FORGET SO MUCH OF CHILDHOOD, BUT WHY? AND why does at least some of it seem like such an important loss?

I was about thirteen when I first realized that there were major parts of my childhood that I could not remember. It was an upsetting discovery, and I remained disturbed about it until the summer of 1995, when I finally began to reclaim what proved to be some truly amazing memories.

One of the profound changes involved in reaching puberty appears to be forgetting many things that younger children take for granted. At that age, I began to be aware that I had, as a younger child, ridden my bike through my dark neighborhood in the middle of the night, for a reason that I had suddenly forgotten. The memory ended as I entered the Olmos Basin, a marshy, heavily wooded flood control area about two miles from my San Antonio home.

During my teens, I found the Basin so disturbing that I couldn't enter it, not even in broad daylight. For years, all I managed to extract from the darkness was the feeling that something terribly important had happened there. When I struggled to remember, I would sometimes glimpse a meaning so incredible that it would leave me gasping, hungering for more—and beating my head helplessly against the wall of seemingly invincible amnesia.

My life has taken some strange turns. The experiences that I have chronicled in my three books about the visitors—*Communion, Transformation,* and *Breakthrough*—have made me question the nature not only of the mind, but of reality itself. My sanity has been at stake. I have denied the truth of my own experiences. I have decided on half a dozen answers ranging from alien contact to a new form of hallucination. Always, I have sensed that those secret childhood nights held the key. It was as if something enormously important—critical, central to everything—was hidden back in those old shadows, and I just could not get to it.

I tried every known way of regaining my lost memories, but all I could ever recall was that I would get on my bike some time after midnight, ride down through my old neighborhood, and go along a path into the Basin. The rest was almost totally blank.

Sometimes I vaguely remembered that a big old tree had been involved, a huge, barrel-shaped thing that reminded me of an African baobab. Under it, or near it, I would meet with other children and with . . . somebody else.

As I matured, the feeling grew that my ordinary

life was not the whole story. It seemed a sort of the-ater, an outer life that concealed another existence that was far more real, far richer, far more impor-tant than this one. In the other life, I had answers to questions about the mystery of man, what is going to happen to us in the future, and who we really are. In this other life, I was a much more powerful human being, and I sensed that this was true not only of me, but of many other people, perhaps of everybody.

But more powerful in what way? What key thing is missing in ordinary life that makes it so . . . ordinary? And, as the years passed, why was I getting a more and more urgent feeling that all this had to change? "Remember who you are" was the catch-phrase of my life. It applies, I suspect, to us all, and the time for us to do it has come.

After I wrote *Communion* and got hundreds of thousands of letters from other people who had also had close encounters, I was profoundly shocked. But what shocked me even more than the letters them-selves was their incredible content. I was not alone in my feeling that something of enormous importance is lost when we leave childhood. Again and again, my readers would mention that they, too, had unremem-bered childhoods. They had been in what I have come to call children's circles, and they also had had mysterious teachers.

Ed Conroy, the author and reporter who wrote a book about my life entitled *Report on Communion,* found other people who had also gone to the Basin in the middle of the night as children, as he reports in his afterword.

But why, always *why*? What did we do? And, above all, why did I feel, more and more, that my life with all its strangeness and pain and improbability— my whole impossible life—was about reclaiming and making known my real childhood?

As it turns out, those memories are the most important thing I've ever known. Now that I am reasonably sure of their content, it chills me to think how close I've come at times to losing them. But I've got a little bit of gold now. I've recaptured some of this lost knowledge.

Although I think that I was in the secret school for most of my childhood, the memories I have recovered so far primarily involve my ninth summer. What I have discovered, I think, is that mankind is living in amnesia, and we don't need to. If this is real—and the evidence, as fantastic as it seems, is compelling—then it represents a window into a deeply secret side of human life, one in which we do things with our minds that are far beyond what has been documented before, but which explain a great deal about why we live as we do.

The nine lessons in this book illustrate one man's journey out of the trap of ordinary life—and it is a trap, make no mistake. Because we do not understand our true past and cannot see our likely future, we are treading close to the edge, very close. If we don't wake up, I fear that we may fall.

I have gained the sense that there exists a science of the soul—perhaps one that we have lost, or never really gained, and that these memories somehow reflect its secret workings. Although I have tried my hardest to make them accurate, they were so deeply buried and are so strange that I cannot be certain that they don't, in some way, also reflect imagination. But that really isn't the issue. This is not a book of simple facts and straightforward claims. It is a mirror, intended to startle you into your own inner recognition.

They shine a light, these memories, straight into the future, deep into the past. They bring understanding to the chaos that is breaking out all around us. They offer a new view of mankind, an entirely new understanding of ourselves, our past, and our future.

Part of the reason that I have remembered these things at this particular time has to do with science. Throughout 1994 and 1995, there were a number of stunning discoveries in areas ranging from archaeology to quantum physics that fit what I was taught when I was nine years old, attending the secret school of childhood. In part because the new discoveries fit the old lessons in so many startling ways, I began to remember.

What I have remembered suggests that the human mind is far more robust than we have ever dared to imagine, and that we can learn to use it in new ways that will fundamentally redefine us and our place in the world. I do not speak simply of new ways of thinking. I am talking about using the mind as a tool that will give us powers that will completely redefine our relationship to time and physical reality.

I remember those days, that magical summer, as if it were still unfolding, that still, hot July forever drifting toward August's deeper thrall. Midnight would come and pass, and here and there—as I am sure still happens today—children would arise and steal softly out of their beds and through their sleeping houses, gliding off into the darkness on their bikes or on foot or on the wings of dream . . . and go to the secret school. I would park my bike near the huge tree, then climb an arrow-straight cut that led up a small ridge to a group of benches and a tiny schoolroom . . . and see a whole hidden world, and taste of a different way of being human.

During the three months of each summer from ages six to twelve, I went to this place. Then the doors were closed to me, and remained so for nearly forty years.

During that period, there were occasional moments when something would come back. Early on, when I was thirteen and fourteen and had just graduated from the secret school, I was in agony but I didn't know why. My memories were blocked. I well recall the tormenting feeling that I had lost somebody who was vitally important to me. I remember begging them to come back, but not knowing who it was I missed. I remember the nights spent sweating it out, tortured by a homesickness that I did not understand, feeling that what I loved the most had been taken from me—and not being able to put my finger on what that was.

Later, there were recurrent dreams of what I called "the dark neighborhood." I am riding my bike in the empty streets, thrilled and frightened at the same time. Then I turn off onto a rocky path, and I meet . . . the dark. Over the years of my adolescence, the homesickness faded and the dreams of the dark neighborhood gradually haunted me less. Every so often, though, something would happen that shook the silent memories and made my heart feel hollow. The most powerful of these events took place in the months before I had the experience that led to my writing of *Communion*.

One clear September day in 1985, I found myself at the Manhattan apartment of a scientist friend, John Gliedman, looking at the single most incredible thing I had ever seen. It was a photograph of a face. Haunting, eerily reminiscent of ancient Egypt, it stared up at me from a desert plain . . . and, incredibly, from memory. "Is this in the Gobi?" I asked Dr. Gliedman.

"Not the Gobi," he replied.

I regarded the image. It reminded me a little of the Sphinx, but there was something harder, more brutal, more primitive about this face. "How old?" I asked. I was beginning to have a very eerie feeling, because it surely seemed as if I could place the thing somewhere in my own past.

"Possibly fifty thousand years. Possibly a lot older."

One thing was clear: this was not the face of somebody at peace. I inventoried my mind—had I seen this in an old book of Egyptian sculpture? In a dream? I couldn't get it to return, not quite. I noticed a mischievous smile on John's face. "This is a joke," I said.

"It's a NASA photo. The face is on Mars."

I was in a completely different mind-set in those days, and my reaction was predictable: "That's the most ridiculous thing I've ever heard." But Gliedman insisted otherwise. He explained to me that the images had been returned by the Viking orbiter in 1976.

I just couldn't believe it. But it was there, and the imaging done by Vince DiPietro and Greg Molnaar was first-class. The worst part of it, the part that was really shaking me up, was that I remembered it. I damn well *remembered* it!

What I did was to just swallow that memory. What was I to think—that I'd been to Mars or somehow seen what was on its surface? Finally, I told myself that I was dealing with some sort of confused childhood memory of the Sphinx. When I was nine, after all, I had suddenly become obsessed with ancient Egypt, hadn't I? I still owned some of the books I'd bought back then.

No matter how I explained it away, seeing the face was still an enormous event in my life, far larger than I could ever have imagined or even—until recently—understood. It may well have been the trigger that caused the close encounter of December 26, 1985, to take place. The mystery of Mars and the secret school, it would turn out, were deeply bound together.

The next thing I knew, I experienced the close encounter that led to the writing of *Communion*, and in the desperate weeks that followed, I forgot all about Mars. I was worried about Whitley. My dread was that I'd had a psychotic episode, possibly brought on by organic brain disease.

That terror was like something alive, a monstrous parasite clawing at my heart. It was a kind of madness in itself. Through all of the chaos and horror of those days, though, there was one single glimpse of something better—a fleeting memory of a time when I was not afraid of this presence that I was beginning to call "the visitors."

This memory flashed past during my second hypnosis session with Dr. Donald Klein, when a window suddenly opened into the secret world of childhood—and it was a very different world from the one I normally recalled.

During the session, something in my tone of voice suggested to the doctor that I had gone back to a period much earlier than the one we were exploring. This sort of spontaneous flashback happens when a traumatic experience that has been repeated through life and suppressed is retrieved under hypnosis. Remembering one event will bring spontaneous recollection of others that were similar.

Under hypnosis, as I was describing an experience that had happened to me while I was alone, I suddenly began talking about seeing other people—soldiers—lying in beds. Dr. Klein later explained to me that he had often observed this flashback phenomenon in his practice, so when he noticed that the change of scene had been accompanied by an alteration in my voice, he asked, "How old were you?"

"Twelve," I was astonished to hear myself answer.

There surfaced at that point a memory of a brief conversation between myself and a visitor whom I appeared, as a boy, to have known well—who, I suspect, was the teacher in the secret school. I ask her who all the men are. She responds, "They're all soldiers." Matters go well until I find that my father is with us, and discover that he is terrified. I tell him it's all right and he says, "Whitty, it's not all right." I can still vividly recall how the terror went through me at the sound of his voice. It felt as if a knife had just sliced my heart in half. Even under hypnosis, even all those years after the incident, the residual fear was overwhelming.

It was at that moment back in the summer of 1957, I believe, that my knowledge of the secret school became suppressed. I suspect strongly that this was intended, that it was part of a large-scale plan that is unfolding not only in my small life, but in thousands of others as mankind comes to the end of this extraordinary age, simultaneously reaching for the cosmos and stepping to the edge of extinction.

That old terror buried a thousand extraordinary memories—buried my recollection of life on a higher plane. I struggled with it in horror novels like *The Wolfen,* about brilliant predators with huge, black visitor-like eyes; *The Hunger,* about strange, immortal creatures that were very much like the tall, blond people I have occasionally glimpsed in my encounter experiences; and *Catmagic,* about a fairy queen and a journey through the world of the dead and back again.

In fact, I believe that my whole body of work— my whole life—has been an unconscious effort to somehow overcome my fears and reach back to the secret school.

I would assume, from the large number of children who are reporting encounters to their parents around the world, that the secret school is very much in session right now, in childhood hideouts all over this planet. But real? *Physically* real? Surely not.

Ed Conroy and I went to the Olmos Basin a number of times looking for the actual location of San Antonio's secret school, but never found it. I assumed that we never would. Then, on November 8, 1995, I made what was for me an amazing and totally unexpected discovery.

TV producer Jim Romanovitch had brought a crew with him from Associated Television in Los Angeles to make a segment about my experiences for a new program they were preparing called *Contact.* Although I explained that there was nothing remaining of the site of my adventures in the Basin, they still wanted to film there.

We went down a familiar path that runs along a streambed that was usually dry, even in my childhood. We saw a huge spider, the place was clogged with cactus, there were anthills, and it became even more amazing to me that any child would come here at night. Then I saw a certain old tree, and for an instant thought that it was the one I remembered. I soon realized that I was wrong again.

Suddenly, I noticed a neat cut angling up from the path, one that I had never observed before. It was old and worn, hardly visible, but still extremely straight . . . and that straightness seemed somehow familiar. I began walking up that way, and, incredibly, this time I did see the old tree—which turned out to be an enormous, profoundly misshapen Texas live oak, its trunk a great black barrel.

My tree. As Romanovitch and his crew filmed, I ran up to it, shouting back to the others. I was overcome with emotion. I hugged the enormous old thing. I then explained, still on camera, that the secret school had been a bit farther along the path, but that we would certainly find no remains. Prattling on about parallel universes, I guided them to where I thought the site must have been.

There were ruins of a wooden structure and possibly a small building, precisely where I had remembered them being. I touched the wood, hardly able to believe my own eyes. Again, my understanding of the world shifted. The secret school was no dream, not by a long shot. This wood was real, this ruined structure was completely physical. It meant that I had come here in the physical world. The strange memories, the dreams of the dark neighborhood—they were physically real.

In many ways, the shock of finding the secret school was even deeper than waking up on the night of December 26, 1985, with the visitors all around me. The last time I had been in this place, I was twelve years old and living inside one of the deepest enigmas in the world. It had been the soft center of a summer night in 1957, in the presence of high adventure and higher mystery. My mind had finally crossed the gulf of amnesia, had enabled me to spot the nearly invisible cut and return to a place that I had assumed lived only in dream.

Then I *really* started remembering. The recollections just came pouring back, and what memories they were. The lessons of the secret school were urgently relevant to our world right now. They implied that we have vast untapped powers of mind that we can make use of right now, just as we are, if only we recognize them.

What a school. Its classes were held in the theater of the unconscious, and buried there, it seems, until the moment when their recovery would be essential. The nine lessons of my ninth summer were structured in three groups of three—a fact that has explained to me one more meaning of the mysterious nine knocks that played such an important role in my encounter experience and that have been repeated in so many lives—even, as I reported in *Breakthrough*, at one point involving an entire town. Like everything else that has happened to me, the nine knocks were a call to memory, one that I have finally heard. I know now what happened after I crossed the dark neighborhood and entered the Basin.

A little boy embarked on a journey into another level of reality during that summer, in his innocence opening the gates of death and leaving the confines of time. Because he was so innocent, he found wonders. With his child's eyes, he could not help but see.

A Child Awakes

There was a child went forth every day,
And the first object he look'd upon, that object
   he became,
And that object became part of him for the day
   or a certain part of the day,
Or for many years or stretching cycles of years.

—WALT WHITMAN

The Coming of the Sisters of Mercy

THE NINTH IS ONE OF THOSE YEARS IN WHICH OUR LIVES seem to anchor. The furies of infancy have died by the ninth year, but the smiles remain; joy is easy to come by and sadness quickly fades. The center of the ninth year is its summer, which is the high summer of childhood.

In the nights of my ninth summer, storms marched, and in their fertile, thundering shadows I participated in the secret colloquies that have—for me—redefined the meaning of the world.

Life in the secret school was a double life, part lived in daytime and ordinary events, part by night and other rules. I remember those days . . .

Flying saucer stories filled the newspapers, science fiction movies were frequent fare at the Saturday afternoon matinee at the Broadway Theater, and my eyes were searching the heavens. I fell in love with the things of the sky, telescopes, and star maps and the curves of night.

My summer in the secret school did not begin with a trip to the Olmos Basin—in fact, it would be weeks more before these journeys actually began—but rather with another experience that is equally beyond explanation. I perceived it as an incredibly vivid dream, but it was far more than that. I would not say that it was a physical experience, but I cannot—incredibly—rule that out. What I do know is that this experience is what lies at the deep, dark center of my being. It is what I remembered when I looked at the Mars face photographs. In that sense, it was like a buried bomb, ticking and waiting to explode into full consciousness.

It took forty years, but what an explosion!

The "dream" concerned Mars. In those days, the newspapers often speculated that the flying saucers might be from Mars, and my father had told me the story of the Orson Welles broadcast of *The War of the Worlds.*

Forty years ago, scientists considered that life on Mars was a serious possibility, and that was where I had focused my imaginings. I can remember making up a game that involved a voyage to Mars, played out in great detail with my friends in a bedroom that we had transformed into a spaceship by covering the windows with sheets. When the game ended, I ripped them down, hoping that our pretense had been so good that we had actually reached Mars. As I stared out across the familiar lawn, the pain I felt brought tears to my eyes. I went silently off by myself.

In the evenings, I used to lie on the roof and gaze with a longing that I could not explain at the shivering dot of palest red that was Mars in the light of the sun.

I just wanted to *go*.

I would look long at pictures of the planet—the vague, furry blurs that were all we had back in the fifties. When I looked, I would dream, and sometimes Mars rolled closer in these dreams and I would see past the fuzzy images into brief clear flashes of a desert plain.

I don't recall anything unusual about the evening of my Mars experience, but it remains the most urgent and extraordinary memory of all in a childhood that was crowded with wonders in the nighttime.

When my memory of it begins, I have succeeded in voyaging out into space, and have found myself high above the surface of Mars. Around me there were reefs and oceans of stars, and I was flying free, unharmed, unhindered, neither frozen by the infinite night nor broiled by the naked sun. Nor did the lack of air make me uncomfortable. Now that breath was gone, in fact, it seemed as if it had been a boundary.

My body sang with the sweet, fierce energy of childhood as I sailed above the empty red desert, regarding with wide-open eyes its remarkable vistas and tasting a delicious sense of great height. But it wasn't all ecstasy. The hollowness that fills children when they are far away tormented me. I could not let myself think about home: I was looking for something and I had to find it because failing would be very terrible. Still, I sure wanted to be home with Momma and Daddy.

The moment I wanted them, I fell. I rocketed toward the surface, the hard, frozen atmosphere billowing my cheeks and blurring my vision. I twisted and clawed and kicked, frantic for some hold, frantic not to lose contact with home . . . frantic to resolve the dream and return safe.

As I dropped, I saw a huge face glaring up at me. I watched for a few moments, transfixed by the glaring eyes, until it resolved into a tumble of low hills.

That one, terrible glimpse, hidden as it was in the depths of my unconscious, would leave me with a fierce obsession—but not with Mars. My obsession concerned Egypt, because what I had seen had looked to me like the face of the Sphinx.

Then the ground was rushing up at me so fast it seemed that I would be shattered. At the last moment, I jackknifed, my muscles howling, the air shrieking, and, with a combined effort of mind, body, and will, made my landing feetfirst and so softly that I barely raised any of the gloomy, dull red dust into the silence of the Martian midday.

I stood absolutely still—a frightened, listening animal. My own clicking breath was the only sound. I looked around me. The horizon was close, the land absolutely featureless, but strewn with sharp, ugly stones and boulders. I could see some hills in the distance, but could not be certain that they represented that terrible face.

When I glanced upward, I gasped, for the sky was tan, rimmed with blue and open at its center to the universe. It looked exactly like a gigantic eye with its pupil full of stars. Not knowing if any of those empty lights were my home, I uttered a whispered, involuntary moan.

All else was so quiet that my own small sigh sounded like the thunder of a restless giant. Such quiet was new to my experience, a soundless sensation completely different from Earth's solitudes. This silence seemed deeper, older, more at one with itself. Even a little boy could taste of it and be moved. It was not an absence but a presence, a noteless, living note.

I tried to find the huge face I had seen, but it was nowhere around. Silence or not, I came to sense that I was being called somewhere and there was not much time. I walked a little, my feet hardly disturbing the soil or the stones. But where to go? Which way? I inhaled the dry air, which smelled like the pulverized iron ore that I'd glued to a card for my rock collection.

Now I heard ticking, and was immediately put in mind of the crocodile in *Peter Pan*. I ran a few steps in no particular direction. Was this ticking a clock attached to some bomb? Had it something to do with Captain Hook?

I could see nothing at any horizon except this flatness and these stones. Feeling very helpless, I began to walk. I went straight ahead, stopping every so often to check my footprints and be certain that I was not circling. I kept hoping that the Sphinx would appear on the horizon, and it would turn out that this was a dream about Egypt.

I felt so *far away*.

Nightmare snarled along the edges of my journey, nightmare lived in this ticking. I moved faster, as fast as

I could short of panic, but the horizon didn't seem to change at all. I felt awful far away and awful lost and this did not want to end.

Now I began to run, even though I feared that it would bring my old enemies, the nightmare men, up behind me with their gray-wrapped faces and long, long arms.

Soon I saw that the horizon was changing. What had been absolutely featureless now displayed a definite swelling. I realized that I was approaching a new tumble of hills, this one on the edge of the huge plain. There were two lines of stones leading straight there, and I was right between them. As I walked, shadows began to crawl out from under the ugly stones. I did not like those shadows, and I did not see how I could bear the Martian night. As far as I was concerned, this might be real outer space, and in *Destination Moon* the space suits needed heaters. I was in a pair of cotton pajamas with nothing on my feet.

My tears froze on my face and my skin seemed to get hard with frost. It certainly felt as if I were really here and I were being killed by this terrible place. But I was also a child, and a child's peerless hunger for life made me struggle even though there was obviously no hope. I fought with the only weapon I had, my mind. "You aren't cold, you are *not*. You can breathe, you *can*. You are not freezing to death and you are not going to die, because this is a damn dumb *dream*!"

The low hill ahead had very regular sides, like something that had been built. This caused me to stop and stare, all my concerns forgotten. The thing could be bigger than the pyramids of Egypt. It might be a pyramid itself.

Without consciously remembering this, I added pyramids to my Sphinx obsession. On my birthday a few days later, I would be taken to Rosengren's bookstore in the Crockett Hotel in downtown San Antonio as a special present, to get any two books that I wanted.

I would choose a book of ancient Egyptian poetry that included a poem five thousand years old, and another of photographs of Egyptian antiquities. I would lie on my bed with my Egypt books and make a telescope of fingers that blotted out everything except the Sphinx, recite the five-thousand-year-old poem in a hush of whispers, and then say to myself, "That was written *five thousand years* ago . . . five thousand years . . . five thousand years . . ." I would imagine myself beside the reedy Nile watching the poet write with his reed pen,

> *He that flieth flieth!*
> *He is no longer in the earth,*
> *He is in the sky.*

I still have those books, after all these years. I have them with me now, and they are helping me, taking me through the dark halls to the deeper part of that night, when the shadow came.

It was late afternoon before I got to the pyramid, which was even larger than I'd thought. It was vast. Its slope was gentle, though; I could walk up the side, which was made of reddish-gray glassy material that looked very much like the ground. I thought, It's camouflaged so it'll be hard to see from above. Something told me that this was part of the problem. I wonder now if Mars was called the Planet of War because it was red like blood, or was there another, more terrible reason?

When I looked back, I was amazed at how high I had gotten. I could see the whole plain I'd been crossing and my own footprints coming from way off. I looked for the Sphinx, but it was nowhere to be seen. There was a sudden dimming of the sun, followed by a shadow sweeping across the plain. I looked up, but could see only empty Martian sky.

However, I was not deceived. I knew that there was something flying around up there, even if I couldn't see it. I got the feeling that it was watching me like a giant eagle, and began to look for a place to hide. The top of the pyramid was only a hundred feet or so farther up, so I went to see if I could find a way in.

What I found was a somewhat flattened area about the size of a football field. There was no obvious entrance, but there was an enormous view. I stared outward, aghast at the size of everything. I was in a whole city of pyramids, and not even on the biggest one. There was another some distance away that looked like it was caved in. A low tumble of hills standing by itself could have conceivably been the Sphinx. If so, it was a lot bigger than I'd thought.

With the sun gone, the sky was filled with stars, so many and so wonderful to see that I shrank back in amazement and some alarm, because for a moment it seemed as if they were so close that they would fall on me. I cannot express the way it felt to behold their multitudes of reds and blues and yellows and pale golds, except to say that I arched my back and clenched my fists and shouted and shouted, a boy's pure cry made faint by the thin atmosphere.

Then, from just overhead, somebody spoke. "We're the Sisters of Mercy, welcome to our school." I cringed away, tried to see enough to run down the side of the pyramid. "Don't be afraid, you darned fool!"

The voice was sort of familiar, and I knew lots of nuns. But Sisters of Mercy? I knew Sisters of Charity of the Incarnate Word and Sisters of the Sacred Heart, but no Sisters of Mercy.

"Sister Euphrasia?" There was a sound overhead then, like the swoosh of her habit as she swept past my desk, and then a soft thud a short distance away. I could sort of see something like a giant bat with a cloak wrapped around it. "Sister?" I wished my voice wouldn't squeak like that, and I wished that it would turn out to be only her.

However, this was not Sister Euphrasia who was here in the dark with me, whom I could not see. This someone had landed, and that was the fact. I hadn't wanted even to think about this, but I knew that it was true. There were Martians all right, and one of them was here.

"At all costs, you will remember the telescope," the voice said. Then a hand came down on my shoulder. "At all costs, you do understand? You will gain access."

"Gain . . . what?"

The voice became a hiss. "You will get to the telescope! You must, do you understand! *Must!*" Her hissing reminded me of the giant lizard at the zoo, the way he hissed when you got him with a mesquite bean.

The hand was weird. It was bony and thin, and it was digging hard into my shoulder. This sure didn't seem much like any dream I ever had before.

Writhing from the pain, I looked up, trying to see this person. But she pushed my head back down and I found myself looking into a huge book made of dark blue leather and crusted with rubies so enormous that I could see my own face reflected in them. I could see the Sister of Mercy, too, a black shadow in the depths of each fat jewel.

Her long, thin hands caressed the cover of the book with the care due a fragile, overripe fruit. And yet it did not seem worn. On the contrary, the sense of antiquity was combined with a quality of the fresh, as if it was both ancient and newly minted.

She lifted the cover, revealing supple, curiously floppy endpapers that reminded me in a creepy way of skin. Instead of pages in the book, there was a strange darkness. I did not want to look; I didn't even want to be near it. Hands grasped my head and pushed it downward. I was aware of sucking, as if the book were a well and there was a creature down there that was going to devour me. I could not prevent it . . . because in some way the creature was also me.

"Now do you see?"

I had shut my eyes as tight as I could. "Nuh-uh!"

Even so, I did. I realized that the book had something to do with my life, future and past. I realized that was why I didn't want to look.

She let me raise my head, and it was a tremendous

relief to get away from it. The air was electric now, a shimmering haze between us. I felt as if I were in some dark trap, not out under these marvelous stars.

"Sister?" I pronounced it "S'ter," like we did in school.

There came a soft chuckle, and without even the faintest sign that the dream was going to end, I found myself back at home in my familiar bed. Bright warm sunlight was pouring in the window at its head, and my little terrier, Candy, was asleep with her muzzle on the pillow beside me. The sweet, familiar perfume of oleander was sweeping in on the morning breeze. I sat up. I was kind of dizzy, but I was so happy to be home that I didn't care. I looked out the window at a sky full of quick little clouds. Doves cooed and mockingbirds sang. At the far end of the yard, our gardener was trying to start the lawn mower, which putted and backfired.

I ran into the bathroom and drank three big glasses of water. After washing my face, I pulled on my summer clothes, which consisted of underpants and shorts, and went racing downstairs to tell Momma and Dad the whole incredible thing.

Then I heard the ticking. I stopped on the landing. I was horrified. It wasn't just my heart, it was something inside me, something *else*. Had I swallowed a clock like the crocodile? No, I'd have noticed. I looked down at my chest.

There—in there—was the solution to the puzzle of the night. I knew, suddenly, that it was the time of the world that was ticking, and that it would not tick forever. It was ticking away.

It still is, and faster.

COMMENTARY ON THE FIRST LESSON

The Mystery of Mars

Obviously, vivid childhood dreams aren't unusual. Even glimpsing a sphinx and pyramids on Mars long before any strange artifacts were actually discovered isn't proof of anything except that, as a child, I was interested both in Mars and Egypt.

There are some things about Mars, though, that are quite strange. For example, according to a *Mutual UFO Network Journal* article of March 1995, by Joseph W. Ritravoto, UFO activity on Earth rises when Mars is closer to us and falls when it is farther away. This is one of the more consistent cycles that the phenomenon displays, and it remained true in the summer of 1995.

On the night of August 1, with Mars retreating, although still close to Earth, 103 people aboard an Aerolineas Argentinas flight landing at Bariloche, Argentina, including both pilots, observed a bright object fly along beside the jet a few hundred yards away. It was described as being as big as the jetliner, and was also observed by the airport tower and military officials. It caused all electrical power at the airport and in the nearby town to fail.

Also in August, an enormous UFO began to be seen over central Colorado in the United States, and by October, there was extraordinary new video from both North and South America. In August, fifteen minutes of tape had been shot in Argentina by a professional TV cameraman, Geraldo Ferraro, who reported that he could see "small windows" in the body of the craft through his telephoto lens. In Colorado, more than six hours of tape had been made by Tim Edwards of Salida, and his father had taken still photographs of a mile-long cylindrical UFO estimated to be hovering at an altitude of sixty thousand feet.

In addition, there were sighting reports from Mexico, Puerto Rico, and South Africa, and tape was shot in all three countries. As of this writing, in May of 1996, the number of sightings has literally exploded, with hundreds of hours being filmed all across the Western United States as part of the most extensive amount of UFO activity ever recorded. This, interestingly, has occurred with Mars behind the sun.

An unexplained observation at Nellis Air Force Base in California of a daylight object was reported by pilots and air traffic controllers. The object was also videotaped, and was remarkably similar in appearance to one that was videotaped over Mexico City in 1994.

In addition to the hours of video amassed since 1992 from all over Mexico by Jaimie Maussan, anchor of their *Sixty Minutes* program, new footage from so many different countries has been made since the summer of 1995 that it is now impossible to deny that there are unknown objects flying around in our skies. So the *Mutual UFO Network Journal*'s March 1995 prediction that the approach of Mars would bring a fresh wave of sightings was absolutely accurate.

Unfortunately, our knowledge of Mars has not expanded much since the Viking mission landed on the surface back in the seventies and obtained the orbital photography that resulted in the discovery of the face. In fact, no attempt to return to Mars has succeeded. In 1993 the *U.S. Mars Observer*, designed to take detailed photographs of the surface, ceased to transmit data back just as it went into orbit around the planet and was lost. In 1988 both Soviet Mars probes, the Prometheus devices, had failed. One of them recorded and photographed the approach of an unknown object fifteen miles long shortly before it was destroyed as it attempted to do an extremely close flyby of the Martian moon Phobos, which, according to some scientists, exhibits many characteristics of a hollow object.

The probes were designed to take photographs of Phobos from as close as a few feet away and to bombard the surface with sensitive lasers, obtaining exact measurements. Together, these two processes would have revealed whether or not Phobos was a structure or simply a stone. The Russians thought that there was a chance that Phobos was not natural, and so had named their probes after Prometheus, who stole fire from the gods.

NASA said that nothing strange approached the Prometheus probe and that the image was a phantom caused by a systems problem. The Russians did not know what it was.

The *Mars Observer* and the Prometheus programs had one thing in common that they did not share with the Viking mission, and that was their extreme sensitivity. Prometheus would have told us for certain whether Phobos is a natural object or an alien artifact. The *Observer* would have been able to detect stones on the surface of the planet the size of a car, and would have solved the mystery of the face.

However, that mystery might be solved before the turn of the century, in any case. NASA plans a number of Mars missions in the next few years. In September of 1997, the *Mars Global Surveyor* moved into a polar orbit around Mars.

While its cameras are not as sensitive as those of the *Mars Observer,* this device is designed to map the entire planet and measure the heights of mountains and the depths of valleys. It is also capable of determining the mineral composition of the surface using an infrared spectrometer.

In early 1998, the first Pathfinder is scheduled to land on Mars and deploy a roving robot and camera. It will be able to measure the elemental composition of the soil and do a small amount of exploration in the immediate area of the landing site.

Later that year, a second Pathfinder will include an orbiter that will send back daily weather reports, a sounding device that will analyze the behavior of volatile chemicals in the atmosphere, and another surface-mapping camera. A lander will explore the high southern latitudes and ice cap.

Beyond these missions, NASA plans to launch two spacecraft toward Mars approximately once every two years.

None of these devices has any particular mission specified involving the Cydonia region and the face. Given the narrow-minded bias toward concealing unusual observations that NASA has displayed since it caught the secrecy bug from all of its Space Shuttle–related associations with the military, it remains to be seen if it will even release genuine results should the face prove to be the artificial structure that it appears or that photographs released will reflect actual conditions on the surface.

Even arch-skeptic Carl Sagan, in his latest book, *The Demon-Haunted World,* grudgingly admits that the Cydonia region is worthy of further study.

In any case, the future will have much to tell us. Could it be, for example, that Mars not only once held life, but that it still does? The Viking lander failed to find life there in the seventies, but it did indicate that, given enough heat, the soil is probably capable of supporting living organisms.

In 1989 and 1990, a group of meteorites discovered on Earth were found to contain signs that they had once been part of a lava flow. They had trapped gases in them that appeared identical to the atmosphere of Mars. This strongly suggests that they were ejected from Mars during a massive volcanic eruption sometime in the last billion years. In 1996, NASA announced that a possible living organism had been found on a Mars meteor.

The new NASA spacecraft will be looking for signs of life. The *Mars Global Surveyor* will look for ancient lake beds and hydrothermal discharge points.

Will they find anything?

Possibly, especially if life on Mars is anything as tenacious as that on Earth.

What about intelligent life? If the face is not a natural formation, then who made it?

Now that's another question. Another question altogether.

LESSON 2

The Angel of the Jails

BACK IN JULY OF 1954, I STILL HADN'T REACHED THE secret school itself. What I knew at this point was that there was someplace I had to go and something I had to do (though I wasn't very clear about what). The thing I recalled most clearly was that I had to get to a telescope and the clock was ticking. I also remembered the Sister of Mercy and the sphinx and pyramids on Mars, but the rest was a jumbled confusion of red landscapes and bursting masses of stars.

The Sister of Mercy was scary. She seemed really old—too old—and I was concerned that she might be a skeleton. Halloweens that I wasn't a pirate, I was a skeleton, because being inside one made them less frightening.

Maybe she was a dead nun who had come out of her grave. I knew about a boy who had supposedly pissed in the sisters' graveyard out behind our school. Could mere knowledge of such a thing be enough to make a skeleton nun come after you?

I asked my mother if there were any nuns from Mars. She said it was doubtful.

I also remembered the sphinx with its staring eyes. Mother said that there was a riddle of the Sphinx, and maybe we could find out what it was if I did some research in the *Encyclopaedia Britannica*. Putting that off, I rode my bike down to the Winn's Five and Ten Cent Store on Broadway about a mile from our house and bought some orange drawing paper, which was the closest thing they had to the color of Mars. I took it home and drew pictures of the sphinx on Mars.

I also drew pictures of the Sister of Mercy, and involved my friends in my speculations about Mars. We decided that Martians would have huge chests because of the thin air. Although I thought they were nuns, I didn't say this because the other kids in the neighborhood weren't Catholics and I didn't want them to get upset that my church had gotten to Mars first.

I began to spend lots of time looking at whatever pictures of Egyptian wonders I could find. I looked for the riddle of the Sphinx in the encyclopedia and stared at the pictures of it in my books. I tried to learn hieroglyphics. I would go up on the roof in the evenings and look for Mars on the horizon.

My nights became troubled. My mother kept seeing a large white owl in the backyard watching the house. She joked to me that it was watching my bedroom. I tried to pay our yardman fifty cents to brick up my windows.

I began to wake up in the night with the feeling that long, bony fingers were touching me. This caused my sleep to become restless, which would soon contribute to some serious problems.

Then I met another angel, this one much more down to earth. I encountered her at the Witte Museum in San Antonio, a week or so after my Mars dream. The museum had an exhibit of shrunken heads that I admired tremendously. They had been brought from the Amazon by my grandparents' friend, Gillard Kargl. The sad peace on those tiny faces was fascinating. In 1994 I learned from Mary Kargl, Gilly's wife, that they had withdrawn the display because they had discovered the heads to be artificial.

On that morning, I had been left to explore the museum while my mother went to a meeting upstairs. I was making nose smears on the case the shrunken heads were in and wondering if I dared lie on the Aztec calendar stone nearby.

"You're not looking, you're devouring," a voice said from far above. I looked up at a tall, bony woman in the sheerest, most complicated, most diaphanous dress that I had ever seen. She wore the largest straw hat I had ever seen. She had big eyes and spoke with the softly cultivated accent of the Old South: there was no Texas edge to her fine diction.

When her eyes met mine, I felt a door get kicked open right in the middle of me. I wished that I had gone to confession and communion and was in a definite state of grace instead of standing here wasting my time thinking how interesting it would be to see them actually shrinking the heads.

She stuck out a hand that looked like it had been shrunken, too. It felt like it was made of dead leaves.

"I am Mrs. Carter. You're Whitty and your mother is upstairs."

"Yes, ma'am."

"Would you care to step out into the garden?"

I applied my best manners to this lady with her high Virginia speech. "Yes, ma'am. Thank you, ma'am."

Behind the museum there was a small patio protected from the broiling Texas sun by big old live oaks. We sat on one of the rock walls that surrounded the patio.

"Well, Whitty, do you think we need a planetarium?"

I wanted to tell her about my planetarium, which could turn my whole room into the night sky. Instead I said, "Yes, ma'am."

"We do," she said. She pointed toward the back of the museum where there were some small cabins that were relics of the settler days. "We could put it over there." She gestured toward the Hall of Transportation.

I didn't comment. The wonder of the idea had silenced me.

"When your mother comes out, where will you go?"

"The club. I'm going swimming."

"Would you like to be in an astronomy class? I have a wonderful telescope."

"Are you a Sister of Mercy?"

We looked into each other's eyes. "Good lord, no." I had no idea that this was an old Texas euphemism for "prostitute." Obviously, Mrs. Carter was not similarly ignorant.

I knew her house, which was huge, but I'd never noticed any telescope. "What kind of telescope?"

"I have a whole observatory on my roof."

"What incher?"

"Four-incher."

By my standards, that was a very nice telescope. "Can you see Saturn's rings?"

"Oh, absolutely."

"The great galaxy in Andromeda? The colliding galaxies?"

Colliding galaxies were an engine of fantasy for me, and I hungered to contemplate the tragedy in firsthand light. People on a planet in colliding galaxies would be able to determine exactly when their world would end, and conceivably do it millions of years before the fact.

"You can certainly see Andromeda."

Now it was time to ask the big question, the one that had dominated since she first uttered the word "telescope." "How about Mars?"

"Sometimes I can see the polar caps. The greening of spring, if the seeing is exceptional."

She was speaking, as far as I was concerned, the language of high magic.

"Does it cost very much money?"

"What?"

"The class."

"Oh, heavens no. Do you know anybody else who'd like to join?"

"All my friends. Plus me."

"We'll have to talk to your mother. Your mother has to give her permission."

That wouldn't be hard to get, I didn't think. "She'll say yes."

"Let's hope," she said.

All of a sudden, swooping down out of the heights in her powdered and gloved magnificence, here came Mother. I was kind of glad, because Mrs. Carter had a way of looking at you that was really amazing. She had strong eyes. They made me think about getting hot and melting like in *House of Wax*, a movie so scary that it had actually made me yell and run off toward the concession stand.

Mrs. Carter stood up. She and Mother faced each other. Mrs. Carter smiled. Mom smiled.

"Thank you for taking an interest, Mary."

"They simply don't know where to put it."

I could see that Mrs. Carter was disappointed. To comfort her, I took her hand, bony or not. I felt her look down at me, then felt her trembling grip and— to my own surprise—suddenly cried out, "Ma-a-an overboard!"

"Whitty!"

"Yes, Momma?"

"Don't be so loud. Mrs. Carter, I'd like to thank you."

Without another word, Mrs. Carter went floating off down the short walk to the parking lot, where she got into a big old car. I could not be sure, but I thought that there was a man in a tuxedo behind the wheel.

We were riding home when I said, "Mrs. Carter has an observatory on her house."

There was no reaction.

"I bet she'd like to have an astronomy class."

"That big old house full of little boys? On the roof? I doubt it."

"She said she would."

We turned up New Braunfels and into the entrance to the San Antonio Country Club. Momma glanced at me. "She's called the Angel of the Jails."

I had no idea what that might be. "Is she a real angel?"

Mother laughed. "Maybe so."

We turned into the club's parking lot and stopped at the entrance to the pool house. I got out, my bare feet smarting on the soft, hot asphalt. Hopping from one foot to the other, I told her good-bye. Then I ran through the pool house and there was our club pool as blue as the sky and full of sparkles and every friend that I had in the world. They were all yelling and laughing.

For a moment, I stood there watching. I was preoccupied with Mrs. Carter and her observatory. Then kids started calling to me to come on in, and I went to my locker to get changed. I loved the chlorine smell of the water and running on the sidewalk and the cool tickle when you first jumped in.

As I was hurrying toward the pool, a shadow crossed the sun. Squinting, I tried to see into the brightness, but there was nothing visible. I looked around at my friends, but they were splashing and laughing and screaming.

Had the Sister of Mercy followed me from Mars? Moving more slowly now, I proceeded toward the water. Everything was so bright, so happy, so very much the way it ought to be. Now, though, I heard the ticking again, and I realized that the problem was not just on Mars, the problem was right here at the club swimming pool, too. The problem was everywhere, and so was the urgent need to solve it.

The ticking echoed off the green stucco walls of the pool house, off the clear water, off the smooth backs of my friends and the blue sky above, and off the frowning edge of clouds in the west.

A storm was gathering there, just along the horizon.

COMMENTARY ON THE SECOND LESSON

Mrs. Carter

I had not thought about Mrs. Carter since I was a child, but as I looked back I began to realize that she was somewhere close to the center of the mystery. When I first remembered her it had seemed as if she was more of a dream-character like the Sister of Mercy. But, like the location of the school itself, she had not been a dream. She had been entirely real.

Who was this woman? I decided to do some research.

Her house still stands across from the old Municipal Auditorium in downtown San Antonio, and the observatory is still on the roof. Through one of my uncles, I came into contact with her son, David Carter, who told me that she had been poet laureate of Texas from 1947 until 1949, an astronomer, and the wife of Judge H. C. Carter. Reading her collection of poetry, *Doubt Not the Dream*, I found in it many uncanny connections to the ideas of the secret school.

The central theme of the secret school is that man can become free in time and space, and that by lifting our eyes, we can gain access to new powers and unlimited promise. This is also the theme of her poetry, and must have been a critical theme of her life.

She wrote:

*Is this wild dream of space, the breaking shell,
man, to free, at last, your dreaming soul?*

Throughout her book, there are references to things like chaos, time, and other matters that were also of primary importance in the school.

Surely it could not have been Aline Carter who was my teacher—the mysterious, sinister, and slightly comical Sister of Mercy? It is odd, though, that I would have associated her in my child's mind with the order, and then written most of this book before I found that she had left behind a volume of poems that reflect the ideas of the school on every page.

I set out to create for myself a picture of Mrs. Carter and her world.

Dressed in the clothing of an earlier age, wearing huge hats, she was a dramatic figure in the San Antonio of the forties and fifties. Old photographs show that she had been a remarkably beautiful girl, with the face of a mischievous little pixie. She had married at sixteen, and Texas artist Eleanor Onderdonk used to say of her that she stayed that age for the rest of her life. When I met her she must have been in her late sixties. With her silks and her hats and her sparkling eyes, I vividly remember the strong impression of mystery that she conveyed to me.

Due to the charitable work she did with prisoners, people called Mrs. Carter the Angel of the Jails. She had saved an outlaw, Pete McKenzie, from execution by proving that he had not shot the police commissioner.

Because of the effort she made on his behalf, even having the commissioner exhumed to prove that McKenzie could not have fired the critical bullet, she was suspected of being in love with the dashing bad man. According to some accounts, she went so far as to furnish his cell with Oriental carpets and paintings. She was the sort of person who inspired hyperbole, however, so the rumors are not too surprising.

As well as being deeply religious, Aline Carter was a scientist. In David's words, "she wanted to show that science and religion weren't at odds with one another."

This, also, has been a major thrust of my own work.

David, an affable man, was quick to invite me to return to the old house, which is still in their family. What, I wondered, would I find down this latest path into the mystery?

As I approached the place, I felt that it was in many ways as enchanted as the secret school itself. It appeared more like something that was asleep than an inanimate object. I thought of Briar-Rose, sleeping the ages away in her enchanted castle.

I raised my eyes to the observatory. Nowadays it would be impossible to see any stars from the center of what has become a huge American city, but in those days the seeing, as astronomers call it, was frequently excellent. When I was a little boy, that small, round structure had been the cockpit of my imagination.

Stars, planets, observatories: these were the miracles of my boyhood, and the four-inch telescope that stood in that observatory had been the most powerful instrument of science to which I had access. I could almost hear my boy's voice piping away up there in the old days, and Mrs. Carter replying in her soft, oddly girlish way.

David unlocked the back door, and he, my wife Anne, and I entered—and it was magic.

Behind the drawn shades and the silence, the old rooms remained as if in thrall, not a stick of furniture moved since long before the days of my childhood. The sense of the past, of its elegance and deep mystery, was incredibly powerful. The light that shone through the shades was soft gold, a light that seemed made of memory. The furniture was Victorian, but spoke also of the real past of Texas, which has much more to do with European culture establishing itself in the wilderness than it does with bad men and shoot-'em-ups.

I looked into the sitting room, toward the spinet that stands beneath the front window. Distantly, I could hear music . . . or could I? Running my fingers up and down the keyboard, I found it to be in reasonable tune.

Coming to this place was incredibly valuable to me. It was as if she had somehow contrived to leave it as a kind of time machine, a ghostly door into the past.

I remembered that there was a fairy chapel with an alcove outside where angels played the harp. These things had always been part of a dream house of mine, a place where Briar-Rose was always just awakening in the fairy chapel and an angel called Melchior strummed her harp in the little round alcove that was her home.

And then I found the alcove, the harp still standing in

it. I approached the small, elegant space. The old harp was no longer polished and gleaming. Its strings were broken, its sounding board appeared to be warped.

It sang to me, though, as it might have when it was whole, and its shadow song filled the tall, still rooms with the grace of times that are gone.

Opposite the alcove was the entrance to the chapel—a small, peaked door. I had certainly been here as a child, but under what conditions? The memories that started trying to emerge were—well, completely incredible. Why was this place so vividly familiar? Why had it been left like this?

Something flitted through my mind—the edge of a memory. I asked David, "Did she lock her doors at night?"

"Oh, no, never. We never did that. Nobody did."

I stood before the entrance to the chapel, wondering when I had last put my hand on this knob, when I had last entered. Painted in its arch is a phrase that I recalled vividly, and which still resonates powerfully in my mind: "Be still and prepare to meet thy God."

I went in. There was a little organ against the back wall, very familiar to me. There were cathedral chairs before the altar, the whole suffused with light softened by golden stained glass.

I moved toward the altar, my whole being filled with wonder. "I prayed in this place," I said. But when? Like the trips to the Olmos Basin, my experiences in this house were curtained by blackness. What had my prayers been? What had I known then that I did not remember now? In those days, I lived in the heart of the secret. Now I am an observer on its distant borders.

How she lingered in her house, in the glow of the chapel, the shadows along the hallways, in the antique elegance of her rooms. I could hear her voice, a quick trill, see her again in one of those marvelous old dresses of hers. David showed us a camphor-wood chest full of silks. We inhaled the perfume and touched the lace, but I chose not to ask what lay deeper within. Perhaps I should have asked to see some of the dresses, but I did not, preferring to leave them as they appeared to me then, flowing with life.

On a tall secretary there lay a magazine from 1922. Inside the secretary there were books within relating to science and religion, silent testaments to her life. And I thought, Here I am, Mrs. Carter, still trying to show that science and vision must combine before either can be whole.

She wrote:

> *I look at earth from distant skies*
> *And wonder, if man knew*
> *The living power that rests in him*
> *Would he dare the unknown too?*

I wonder, also. I wonder who she really was, the Angel of the Jails.

She was a known person, certainly, a minor figure in Texas history. She was the daughter of the first Anglo-American born in the state, a child of the Western frontier and child-wife of a wealthy lawyer.

Growing up here during the years of the Old West, she would have remembered the dust that the cattle drives raised as they went down the street that is now called Broadway, heading for the Chisholm Trail. She knew outlaws and was not afraid to concern herself with humble people.

She wrote:

> *He had no name,*
> *Or so the crowd thought as they passed him by,*
> *But at night when he lay on an old park bench*
> *He looked through the trees at the star-filled sky.*

Had I found in her the identity of the cowled figure who brought wisdom so novel to my child's mind that it seemed to me to come from another world?

David then led us to the telescope, up through the large room at the top of the house that they always called the ballroom.

It was full of boxes and dusty furniture now, and had never been grand enough to be a real ballroom. I could hear music, I could *feel* dancing, as if my body bore memories that I could not access. I knew, though, that dancing had been a big part of my life in the secret school, my life with the visitors, dancing in the moonlit nights of long ago . . .

Then we ascended the narrow stairs to the roof, and there was the observatory just as it had been when I had last seen it thirty-seven years ago. I remembered every step I had taken to reach it, my struggles with the mechanism, then entering the dark interior and reading by the pale moonlight the words painted around its circumference: WHEN I CONSIDER THY HEAVENS O LORD.

I remembered looking up at the night sky, trying to

figure out how the spotting scope would work, aiming it, pressing my eye to the eyepiece.

And then, just like the trips to the Olmos Basin, there was darkness. The memory ended, cut off clean.

I laid my hand on the humble old instrument, touching the dull barrel that once had gleamed with starlight. A breeze came up, and the tops of nearby trees spoke softly to me of the past, of childhood, and the secrets of those days.

The Man in the Lightning

THE EXTRAORDINARY THINGS THAT HAD HAPPENED TO me so far that summer—my dream of Mars and the need to reach a telescope, then meeting Mrs. Carter with her promise of access to one—served to lead me closer and closer to the secret school.

I was passionate, at this point, about getting to that telescope. But I could not simply go down to her house. It was a long trip downtown, one I'd never done before by myself. I had to get permission, above all to make her follow through on her promise of an astronomy class. I had to *do* something.

Once I had reached this level of urgency, the real introduction to the secret school began, outside and at night. I didn't know it, but what was necessary now was to face my fears. I was on a quest, and the first part of any quest is the battle with the monster.

We had sleep-outs where we would shine flashlights at the sky and try to get a flying saucer to land. Then we would hide in our bedrolls, such as they were. I would say the Our Father and the Hail Mary in case they showed up. If they did, we planned to ask for an "interociter," which was the faster-than-light communications device shown in a film that had just recently captured our space-happy imaginations, *This Island Earth*.

After I'd been brought home from swimming on the day I met Mrs. Carter, my friend Albert came over. We retired to the deepest, best shade under the pecan tree, breathing its piquant scent and talking of distant worlds and starships, and what it might be like inside, what the seats would be like and the living rooms, and what dishwashers and fans were like on Mars and beyond. We concocted gravity drives and light drives, and imagined how the pilots might navigate by measuring the ebb and flow of redshift among the stars.

I thought that the spacemen would look very strange, with eyes big enough to see in the dark of space. I made up a language for them, which was a mixture of Spanish songs like "La Cucaracha" and the most solemn church hymns, all sung while barely moving your mouth.

When the light grew long and the air got cooler, we bestirred ourselves and played at flying down the frontyard hill and seeing how long we could make our shadows get. I tried to see if my shadow traveled at the speed of light. Could I get it to stretch all the way to Mars?

We had an old war-surplus pup tent that we used for sleep-outs. Pup or not, it was easily big enough to shelter six or seven kids buried in an indeterminate mass of sheets and blankets. After supper, we hauled it out into the vacant lot behind the house. "The lot" was a prime playground for us, where wars were conducted, victories celebrated, forts constructed and destroyed, and hide-and-seek was played. In the part where the weeds grew taller than the tallest of us, we faced the mysteries of Lost Land. All our wars revolved around the same issue: which side had to be the communists. Since nobody ever lost, it was never resolved.

We were just unrolling the tent when I realized that I could see a pale red star through the trees. I stopped, transfixed. It felt as if the light of Mars was shining down into me, as if it was living light, as if it knew my name.

I dropped my end of the tent and took a few steps away from the others. "Hey," Al said.

"He's having a crazy," my sister said.

"He always has his crazies when there's work to do! I don't call that very crazy," Al replied.

"Oh, he's very crazy."

"Your momma says he's gonna be a writer."

"What can she say—that he's going to be a lawyer or an oil man? Him?"

I could hear the voice of the Sister of Mercy saying "remember, remember," and I could feel the ticking urgency as if it had become part of my blood. I burst into tears. My sister came and put her arms around me as I fought to control myself. "Patricia, do we know the future?"

"Nobody does. Only God."

I went back to the tent, and soon we had it up pretty good between its posts. It was dark now, and Al and my sister seemed to me to be glowing with more than just moonlight. They looked very beautiful to me, which was also kind of scary, because I had never seen them in this way before.

Then we heard adults. Albert's father was here and he was calling him from the driveway. His car lights were shining so strongly along the drive that they made the backs of scurrying sow bugs gleam like little diamonds.

"Al, I want you home tonight."

"Oh, Dad, no!"

My father came down the walk from our kitchen. Inside, our cook and maid Annie was washing up, and I could hear the dishes clinking. Daddy was still in his suit, and a cigarette glowed between his fingers. "Evenin', Leon."

"Karl, I don't think the kids should be out tonight."

"Well, it's a pretty night for it." Dad had a low voice that could sound to me like the voice of God. He was a stocky man with his hair combed straight back from his forehead, and everything he did and everything he said was, I felt, extremely important.

Both men gazed off toward the lot. They regarded the heat lightning on the horizon. I knew, suddenly, that Al's father was afraid. Had Al told him about our plans to call the spacemen? Was it dangerous or something? I didn't quite understand. Wasn't the whole point to get them to land?

Al was taken home, fighting tears. But soon I heard

my other best friend, Mike, calling our special call, a high, wailing sound that was intended to be as eerie and chilling as the fabled Rebel yell.

We were already building a fire when Roxy and Angie's dad brought them. Roxy was almost as tall as Patricia. She had black hair, creamy skin, and was quiet. Angie was two years younger, blond and pudgy and full of laughter. Quiet or not, Roxy would eagerly join in any kind of trouble that could be devised.

Full night came, and I huddled around our fire with my friends. We pretended that it was freezing cold and that the lightning bugs were snowflakes. Every once in a while they'd swirl, which was pretty, but also meant that the wind was getting up. At a certain point, all the heat lightning and the wind would make our parents decide that there were going to be storms later and we'd be called in, just like Al.

We were behind the honeysuckle hedge that separated the lot from our backyard, and the air here was heavy with the scent of the flowers. Small, pale clouds of the kind that we called ice clouds swept up from the south, so low that it seemed you could hit them with a rock.

Our fire crackled. We roasted marshmallows and tried to pop popcorn, but it caught on fire. Down in the yard, the adults talked softly together.

We were laughing and yelling and running around with burning marshmallows on sticks when one of the adults started singing in a voice so beautiful that we all fell silent. He sang, "I'll take you home again, Kathleen, tho' the ocean be wide and wild," and the song pierced the heart.

I raised my eyes and saw that the storm on the southern horizon had grown and was now flickering with continuous lightning. As I watched, a somber mountain of cloud slid upward, obscuring the light of stars.

Katydids conducted their somnolent arguments in the trees, and somewhere in the depths of the moonlight a mockingbird trilled on a wire. Mort and Joe, the overbred and half-crazy springer spaniels owned by our next-door neighbor, set up a howl.

"There are ghosts out tonight," Mike said.

Angie clapped her hands over her ears and yelled, "It's against the law to talk like that!"

"Ghosts with long, sharp teeth," he added.

Mike was older than me by three years, and the object of my great admiration. He could hold his own in fights with the girls, which in my eyes made him extraordinary. Also, he had a marvelous imagination and could think up all sorts of games. He was perfectly informed.

"You know it when the dogs howl. They can hear the gnashing."

"It's the storm," my sister said.

I did not want to be scared so badly that I would have to go in, so I put my fingers in my ears. Mike came close and said, "The ghosts have snaky fingers and great big eyes like owls." He paused. "They're real," he whispered.

Then he jumped into the tent and buried himself in our blanket pile. It was about nine when the rest of us went into the tent. Dad came out and double-checked that our fire was properly damped with earth. He told us he didn't think it would storm, but if it did we'd be fine if we just stayed in the tent. This really surprised us, because normal operating procedure was to make us come in at the least hint of a storm, and the condition of the sky more than hinted.

Soon Dad's footsteps crunched off through the brush. The porch light went out. I felt as if we'd been sealed up in a tomb.

"Tick-tock," Mike sang, "the end of the world. Tick-tock, the end of the world."

"You ever been to Mars?" I asked. But my hunch was wrong because he looked at me as if I were completely insane.

Roxy and I tried to have a farting contest, but it did not come to anything even though we stood on our heads and almost wrecked the tent. Then we all sang "Ninety-nine Bottles of Beer." Roxy, Mike, and I had a whisper and made secret plans to sneak out later. The three of us had a very, very secret club that sneaked out at night and met in the middle of New Lost Land, a swampy area at the end of the block with eight-foot-high johnsongrass and lots of snakes. Sometimes some of us took off our clothes and crept through the neighborhood naked.

On we journeyed, deep into the night. We no longer discussed our idea of calling flying saucers down. Privately, I wished we'd never even thought of it.

We must have fallen asleep about midnight, but I did not sleep well, waking up every half-hour or so. Finally, I sat up in bed. The tent was completely quiet. The silence outside told me that it was very late. I had learned that when the katydids went to sleep, it was always after midnight, the time my parents called "the wee hours." When somebody died, people always seemed to say, "He just slipped away during the wee hours." It was the time when Death walked, Mike had explained.

Bright, silent flashes flickered through the tent walls, and I realized that I had been awakened by far-off lightning. I looked toward the door. Should I open it? Dare I? The flickering was everywhere, and I had never seen anything like it. I crawled closer.

Finally I untied the fasteners. But still I hesitated. What might be out there, what electric creature? I wished that I'd never dreamed of the Sisters of Mercy, never noticed the shadow that had crossed the sun at the country club. I wanted to be inside the house under my own covers, cuddled up with Candy and with my own policeman with a gun to protect me.

The flashes came again, brighter than ever, and this time I thought I heard a distant grumble of thunder. Finally, I thrust my face out into the night.

What I beheld entered my eyes, but made no sense. Then it resolved itself, and I opened my mouth but did not—could not—cry out. Instead, a low sound escaped as I slowly drew myself out of the tent and stood up and faced the tremendous sky.

Towers and towers of clouds filled its whole southern half, stretching from horizon to horizon. My skin prickled as I listened to the same living emptiness that I had heard on the surface of Mars. Although the clouds were lit as if by racing creatures of fire, some trick of wind was stopping the thunder.

From the rail yards down near the center of town the night train's whistle began to wail. The Southern

Pacific overnighter was pulling out on its way to New Orleans.

Of the storm, I thought: it's another world. Below it was the sweet, familiar land of South Texas: Yorktown of my father's birth; Pearsall, where Mr. Cassin had his ranch; Eagle Pass, where we hunted the white-tailed deer; Yoakum and Refugio and dreamy old Indianola, where my great-grandmother had first set foot in Texas.

South Texas dreamed as the other world swept past above, castles and cliffs rising to the stars. I could imagine electric people living at light speed in the storm. Their lightning wars would be fought in an instant; their whole histories would rise and fall in a flashing hour.

The other world came swiftly and softly closer, and now I could hear its grumbling, now smell the wild smells of the vast rangeland over which it was sweeping. What I could not understand was the suddenness of its coming, the way the long fingers of cloud seemed to reach out over a course of only moments and envelop us, the way its thunder opened as if a stone had been rolled back, and suddenly the trees were tossing and the sky was roaring.

Then the rain swept across the sleeping town, drowning the wail of the night train and driving me back into the doorway of the tent. Behind me my friends slept in warmth while all around the gray rain pounded.

A sizzling ball of lightning came bouncing up through the lot, speeding across the tops of the tall grasses. I'd never seen ball lightning, and was amazed by the round structure and swarming fire inside. Popping like chicken in a skillet, it burst into a million stars and was gone, only to be replaced by another. Then three more came down out of the clouds, sinking with the sad grace of kites that have lost their strings.

These also came bounding down, bouncing on the ground and then arcing high overhead. In the center one I saw the outline of a man. He was blurred in the fire, but I could definitely see him. His body was naked and he had his fists against his temples and his mouth was open. I couldn't hear a sound, but the anguish in his face reached me and I clenched my own fists and groaned. Then I heard his voice, very faintly, the man who was trapped in there. He was howling and it was as lost a sound as I have ever heard, as if he had been deprived of everything he knew and understood and left only with his terror. As the ball swept closer, the cries got louder.

I saw that it was going to hit the ground about fifty feet in front of me, and it did hit and I could smell its electricity, a vibrant odor. I held my hands to my head and crouched, but the ball got bigger and bigger still, and finally was like the sun blazing in my face. It felt as if I could sense with the man's senses and taste of his terror, and what I felt was that I was lying in the arms of monsters in a stuffy little chamber in some lost nowhere of the mind and I could not make myself wake up and I could not make them let me go and I was so dreadfully afraid, so terrified that I had lost all nature—human nature, animal nature—and had become fear unbound.

I turned to run back to the tent, and then heard over and over, in addition to the wailing, other voices that sounded like the voices of my sister and my friends saying, "What can we do to help you stop screaming?"

Many years later, I would describe something very similar in *Communion,* as I reported on the events of December 26, 1985: "One of them . . . said, 'What can we do to help you stop screaming?'" It's almost as if the man in the ball of fire was me doubling back through time in some incredible attempt to escape . . . or a strange childhood nightmare that boiled up again many years later.

Opening my eyes, I found myself back in the tent's sticky dark. Outside, the rain hissed. Here and there, busy drips pattered on our blankets. From time to time, the canvas shuddered and thunder rolled heavily in the night.

I sat up, then crawled to the door of the tent and once again lifted the flap. It was really pouring, the wind whipping nearby sunflowers and hissing in the honeysuckle hedge. When there was lightning, I thought I could see a hazy shape standing in the glare.

It was warm in here but I knew it wasn't safe. This was just a little tent and we were alone in the lot in the middle of the night. I had seen the man in the ball of fire. As far as I was concerned, the world of my dreams was very real, and right outside.

"We have to go to the house," I said. "We have to because of the storm."

The storm seemed about to break the whole world in half, and a cold, wet gust came under the edge of the tent and puffed its walls out until the stakes almost came up. Some years later, a storm would blow our tent down completely, but all this one did was soak us.

All the kids ran and I ran, too, but they got to the house faster. As I came up to the broad, screened porch that stood across the back of the house, the yellow bug lights inside went on and I could see my friends starting to make a hut by draping towels over the big picnic table we had out there. When we wanted to be safe but also in the rain, we made a storm hut under that table. The rain would be all around you and blow in gusts through the screen, but you stayed dry.

I ran up to the screen door but could not open it. Somebody had locked me out. I started crying and pounding until my sister finally came out of the storm hut and unlatched it. Although we fought a good bit, we also loved each other and would stick up for each other whenever the neighborhood turned against one of us.

I don't remember much about that particular storm hut, but I don't think that we had fun. Soon though, with the grace granted to the young, we slept.

In my dreams, Martians came in and sat around on the redwood porch chairs and talked quietly among themselves. Without their wimples covering their heads, the Sisters of Mercy had big wrinkly craniums with white hair and empty eyes and necks as thin as corn stalks. They moved their long arms when they talked and waved their snake fingers in the air, and their night-black claws gleamed.

The next morning, my obsessions intensified. The ticking became continuous in my head, and I felt that I had to get to Mrs. Carter's telescope right away.

If only she would set up her astronomy class. Why didn't she go ahead and do it?

Days passed. I hinted to my mother, but nothing came of it. Finally, I began to think that Mrs. Carter had done what adults usually did, and forgotten her promise.

I waited for the evenings, when I would go up on the roof and stand at attention on top of the chimney, gazing in the direction of Mars.

COMMENTARY ON THE THIRD LESSON

The Mystery of Time

That strange incident came to the surface of my memory one day when I was thinking about another, similar sleep-out that I reported on in *Communion*. I was trying to use my memory of this later incident to enable me to recall the earlier night of ball lightning, which I sensed had been at least as important, and probably more so.

That was an accurate hunch, as it was the culminating lesson in the triad of lessons that formed the foundation of the summer's studies. It revealed their aim, which was breathtaking. What I would learn next was nothing less than a new way of addressing reality, one that did not rely on linear time or ordinary space.

Of all the things that have happened to me, the true nature of which has often been so difficult to distinguish, the series of memories from the secret school involving time, movement in and out of time, and actually living outside of time appear to me to be the most compelling evidence of there being an actual contact in my experience with aliens or an advanced mind of some sort.

Even so, I do not find bizarre experiences in time like this too surprising, because I am aware of the many thousands of readers who have written me describing such effects in their own lives. More than one encounter witness has seen so much of his past and future life that he has ended up living in a permanent state of déjà vu.

Altered time has been a feature of encounters from the beginning. Among the earliest modern encounters are reports of strange experiences with time and statements from the visitors to the effect that we don't understand time.

In Jacques Vallee's masterpiece *Passport to Magonia,* in which he describes the intricate relationship between ancient myth, fairy lore, and modern encounter testimony, there are recounted many instances of similar temporal distortions that predate the modern era. Time speeds up, as in the case of Wang Chih, who paused to watch some strange old men playing chess and found that centuries had passed while he was there. Celtic fairy lore is full of stories of people dancing in fairy rings, only to find that hours, days, and even years pass, seemingly in a few minutes. The modern encounter experience mirrors this phenomenon.

On October 15, 1957, Brazilian farmer Antonio Villas-Boas had an intense close encounter that involved being taken aboard an apparent spacecraft while in normal consciousness. After a sexual contact of a type that has since been reported many times, he was left with extensive physical side effects that were examined and documented by a doctor, Olavo Fontes, who was a professor at the Brazilian National School of Medicine.

Dr. Fontes confirmed that Mr. Villas-Boas was not psychotic, and that his physical side effects, including nausea, sleeplessness, and the radioactivity of parts of his body, were entirely real.

Toward the end of his encounter, Mr. Villas-Boas had attempted to steal what appeared to be a clock, but was prevented by his abductors. This strange device had markings that corresponded to the three, six, nine and twelve positions, but only one hand, and the hand did not move.

When he was at length returned to the field from which he had been taken, he was surprised to discover what has since become a commonplace of the experience: he could not account for all the time that appeared to have passed.

In 1961, witness Betty Andreasson observed her whole family become paralyzed, as she put it, "as if time had stopped for them." Under hypnosis, Betty has said that "they can reverse time." Her experiences have been extensively reported in a series of books by researcher Raymond Fowler, beginning with *The Andreasson Affair*.

In 1970 another witness was told that we don't use time correctly and that it could be speeded up, slowed down, even stopped. Interestingly, this witness, a Wisconsin attorney, was also told that they traveled faster than light and that we couldn't visit them because of our *ideas* about time. This case was reported in 1976 by Warren Smith in *UFO Trek*.

During the world-famous encounter of Betty and Barney Hill memorialized by John Fuller in his 1966 book *The Interrupted Journey*, it was reported that Betty Hill had been asked many questions about time. Among them were "What is old age? What is a year?"

To what extent is time travel *really* possible? What do we actually know about this? Over the past few years, there has been an enormous change in theoretical physics regarding the possibility of time travel. In 1993 renowned physicist Dr. Stephen Hawking dismissed it. He said that the best evidence that it didn't exist was that "we haven't been invaded by hordes of tourists from the future." Unless, of course, we have simply failed to recognize them.

In October of 1995, he revised his position: "One of the consequences of rapid interstellar travel would be that one could also travel back in time."

It has always been assumed that the universe would somehow bar journeys back in time, no matter how compelling the mathematics of the situation. This was because of the so-called grandfather paradox. You could not go back and marry your grandmother, thus becoming your own grandfather. And therefore, the thinking went, you couldn't go back at all. However, it has been convincingly postulated by Russian physicist Igor Novikov, who first proposed the grandfather paradox, that a known force in physics, the "principle of least action," will prevent this paradox. The principle of least action means, simply, that nothing will consume more energy than it must. A seed dropping from a tree will go no faster than gravity makes it. A stone tossed in the air will never rise higher than the amount of energy put into the effort allows.

Novikov applied this principle to time travel and, in a brilliant feat of mathematics, disclosed that the only movements through time that satisfy the principle of least action *must be* those in which the grandfather paradox cannot apply.

In other words, time travel will never cause a situation in which one of these paradoxes could take place. If you might indeed seduce your own grandmother, you will never meet her.

According to John Gribbin in the *New Scientist* of August 12, 1995, the latest scientific thinking is that "there is nothing in the laws of physics to forbid time-travel." But what would it actually entail? Would we need to build time machines, and if so, what would fuel them and what would it be like to sail in them down the river of time?

What we would need is access to a particle stream that was moving faster than light. The faster something travels, the slower its subjective time passes in relation to the rest of the universe. Faster-than-light travel results in backward movement through time.

Where would we find such a thing, let alone gain access? Certainly such particles exist: there is a straight-line stream of particles pouring out of the stellar object Cygnus X-3 that must consist of neutrons. Since neutrons have a half-life of only fifteen minutes and we can see them although they are light-years away, they must be accelerated to faster-than-light speed. If we could harness them, we could use them in some way, perhaps to sail physically backward in time or shine them like a beam into the past.

A time machine would not be a mechanism of gears and wheels, nor even one of circuits and processors. In a sense, it might be easier to create one than we have realized.

Could the mind somehow enable time travel? If it is nonlocal in nature—that is to say, not confined to ordinary space-time—there might be a way as yet not understood for it to address time through the medium of faster-than-light energies.

Such energies are already being utilized in scientific experiments. In April of 1995, a paper was published in *Science* claiming that hyper–light speed had been used in an experiment that played a brief portion of Mozart's *Jupiter* Symphony.

A big part of the secret school appears to have been devoted to giving us a taste of how states that enable time travel, prophecy, and psychic activity feel so that we could return to them later. I have personally experienced many movements through time, and it appears that such things are, while not commonplace, certainly far from unique.

In March of 1983, I was standing at the corner of La Guardia Place and Houston Street in Manhattan when a most remarkable event transpired. There was no warning at all. I did not feel in any way unusual.

At the time, I was working on *Nature's End* with Jim Kunetka, and I was steeped in information about the future, most of it pretty distressing. Although such a thing was not on my mind, a journey to the past would have been a welcome relief.

I had gone out to take a walk and clear my mind. It was a gray, cold day, and I was planning to cross the street and proceed up to Broadway. As I began to cross toward West Broadway, I stopped because the pedestrian light was blinking DON'T WALK. In New York, the pedestrian lights blink before they actually change, but as Houston is a very wide street, I decided to wait through the red light until it was full green again.

In that moment, as I stood on the curb, I heard the clip-clop of horses and a great cacophony of creaking and sloshing directly in front of me, as if there was some large, invisible wagon passing no more than a foot in front of my face.

I stepped back, not yet understanding what was happening, and turned toward movement that caught the corner of my left eye. There then became visible, as it wheeled around the corner, a tall wagon pulled by enormous dray horses. It was green and lined with big black barrels that sloshed as it clattered along. On the side was a gold-lettered sign reading GOULD. I could smell pickles.

I thought that it was some kind of a promotional stunt, until it passed and I saw that the Silver Towers, twin twenty-story condominiums across the street, had entirely disappeared and had been replaced by brownstone row houses.

Turning back, I saw a whole panorama of change. Coming up West Broadway was a group of five or six men on horseback. They wore red cutaway coats, black boots, and derbies, and appeared to be riding very good horses. They were turning east on Houston Street.

The change was shockingly real, and my first impulse was to turn around and run back home, but every time I made the least movement, a horrible sensation entered the lower part of my body, as if ice-cold water were pouring through me. This drew me to look down toward my waist, whereupon I saw a bit of newspaper lying in the gutter at my feet. Instinctively I reached toward it, only to find that any movement caused the horrible, icy feeling to spread up my body.

At that moment, the thought crossed my mind that if I touched that newspaper, I would be completely and utterly unstuck in time, lost. That ice was the past clutching at me with its cold hands, seeking to make me part of itself.

I froze, terrified, and then heard a distinct sound beside me—a choked, feminine gasp.

Carriages and wagons were beginning to clatter past and the air was filling with strange smells to add to the diminishing reek of the pickles. A toasty scent of coal smoke and something like rotted fruit predominated. The intimate details of the past were taking my consciousness over. the DON'T WALK sign seemed a million miles away, a thin and fading dream. My present life felt like something I had imagined.

I turned toward the gasping sound and a small woman, elaborately dressed in black, went skittering away from me. Then I heard a shout from across the street, the voice rising sharply above the clatter of traffic.

A menacing man stood there, his derby down on his eyes. He was shouting at me, his voice taut with fear and questioning. I think that he was frightened and upset, probably because of my strange dress (I was wearing casual clothes—an open shirt, a sweater vest, and a leather jacket), which would have appeared very out of place to him. My loneliness actually hurt, it was so intense. I do not think I could have borne it a moment longer.

Then the past seemed to fall on its side, as if it were a stage set that had been shoved away. And then it was gone. As suddenly as it had become real, it transformed itself into a memory again. It was as if it simply changed places with the present. It was as smooth and easy as a set change in a well-equipped theater.

Amazingly, the DON'T WALK light was still blinking. The whole incident had taken only a few seconds, no more, even though it had seemed to last easily five to ten minutes.

Was it real? I went so far as to go to the public library and check the newspaper collection for the 1870s and 1880s, reading the old *New York Journal* on the theory that this rather sensationalistic paper might have featured a story about an oddly dressed man who had disappeared off a street corner.

I found nothing, but I did discover a story from 1945 about a woman dressed in black who suddenly lurched into the middle of Forty-second Street, seemingly from nowhere, then disappeared. In addition, I tracked down a rumor from the mid-seventies about a group of people who had gone out of an office building on Madison Avenue and had, upon reaching Fifth a block away, seen a pyramid where the New York Public Library was supposed to have been.

I spoke to one of these people, a woman who had been a secretary on Madison Avenue at the time. She remembered seeing not a whole pyramid, but a sort of double exposure of what appeared to be the bottom part of a pyramid with sloping stone sides and a small door of Egyptian appearance. It was superimposed on the east front of the Main Library.

She had no idea what it had been. It was there, as far as she could remember, for about ten minutes. Quite a number of people had noticed it. She'd said that she thought it was some kind of reflection, but later, when people at the office had discussed it, had realized that it was what she described as a "stone ghost."

She did not know what she had seen, but I knew the structure well. It was not a pyramid. What she had observed was some sort of extratemporal ghost of the side of the old Croton Receiving Reservoir, which had been constructed with an Egyptian motif and had been torn down to build the library toward the end of the last century.

I polled a group of my friends almost at random and discovered the following: one woman remembered an incident in which she and her boyfriend had been traveling down a highway in a Camaro when they found themselves on a narrow, two-lane road that appeared to be the same highway some time in the forties or early fifties. She was asleep when the incident took place, but her boyfriend was deeply shocked. He'd barely been able to keep the car on the road.

In another incident, a man had left the center of a crop circle in England to discover that he couldn't find his car. He went along the road until he saw a village in the distance. He was appalled to realize that it did not appear to be a modern place. He'd gone back into the sixteenth century. He rushed back to the circle to get the others who were there, but never saw the village again.

A third woman, an attorney, had once seen what appeared to be a gigantic dinosaur crossing a highway, but it disappeared into nothingness as her car approached it.

My guess is that such experiences are commonplace, and the reasons that this would be so are becoming more clear. It could be that time does not flow evenly, but rather more like an uneasy river with currents and rapids and eddies, which on occasion cause these events.

While I do not want ever to assert without proof that this *must be* time travel that I'm describing, there was nevertheless a flavor to my own personal experiences that suggests strongly to me that I was dealing with something real.

Perhaps, when unknown lights sail the night, we are seeing ships from future skies. Perhaps the aliens in our dark bedrooms are our own grandchildren's grandchildren, come back to trigger the very evolution of consciousness upon which their existence depends, even to seek fertilization from our still-fecund era. After all, the human sperm count has apparently been dropping for years in many countries. If the trend has been correctly measured—and there is some controversy about that—it could mean that the average male will be infertile by 2015. So maybe all of the sexual activity that I and other witnesses observe involves the harvesting of fertile sperm and eggs by people from a barren human future.

There exists a small possibility that time travel was

understood better in the past than it is now. Among the very oldest of Egyptian priesthoods was the Society of Horus, whose job it was to send the dead pharaoh back in time to the period of the first king, who would then enable him to ascend into the constellation of Orion and become immortal.

What this may signify mythologically is obscure, but if it is taken as fact, then it means that the dead man was conveyed into the past, where there existed the technology to resuscitate him and take him on an interstellar journey.

In any case, the Egyptians certainly had the concept of time travel, and believed that they could accomplish it. Such thoughts never crossed my mind when I was nine. I soon forgot the face in the lightning. What I could not forget, though, was the sense of urgency. The ticking of the clock had become part of me.

Somehow, I had to get to Mrs. Carter's telescope.

But before I could at last embark on that adventure, there was a dramatic interruption, one that nearly ended the whole story.

The Telescope

He that flieth flieth!
He is no longer in the earth,
He is in the sky.

—"THE DECEASED'S JOURNEY"
FROM THE PYRAMID TEXTS
TRANSLATED BY JOSEPHINE MAYER
AND TOM PRIDEAUX

Eddie Death

MORE THAN ANYTHING, WHAT STANDS BETWEEN mankind and freedom is the fear of death. But how could a child on what was so far nothing more than a quest to reach a certain telescope possibly find that such a great fear stood in his way?

The secret school wasn't about astronomy. It wasn't about telescopes. It was about a true vision of mankind. Between me and the revelation was a wall, and the bricks were fear. On the other side of that wall was the land of the dead.

The morning after the storm was clear and very still. We got up before dawn, returned to the lot, and made a fire, shielding its glare from the house with an old piece of tin roofing. Then we fried eggs and bacon, and had a breakfast that I remember as being more or less completely black.

The sun rose, and we went through the backyard looking at the spiderwebs that had revealed themselves in the dew. Nothing was said of the alarms of the night.

That afternoon I felt bad, and by eight I had a fever. All that night, I was sick. By the next morning my skin was baking like a summer street and there seemed to be plaster dust coating the inside of my mouth. I could look up through the top of the window at the head of my bed into the green glowing leaves of the big old mesquite tree out there. I watched a squirrel jump from one limb to another. I drifted with the cooing of the doves and the lazy howl of the cicadas.

"How'd I get so sick?" I asked the silence. Candy was curled up beside me, and when she heard me speak I could feel her stub tail wag against my thigh. I put my hand on her. Momma came in and set a damp washcloth on my forehead. I gazed at her in her red-and-white-checked dress and regarded her smooth arms as she tucked in my sheets. Her eyes touched mine. "How'd I get so sick, Momma?"

To my surprise, she hugged me, lifting me off the bed and pressing me against her. Then I heard my father's voice downstairs, which surprised me further, because it was already late morning. "Why's he still here?"

Instead of answering me, she stuck the thermometer under my tongue. While we waited for it to register, she stroked my cheek with her soft hand, which felt very nice and made me close my eyes. I realized that I was lying on the bed with no covers. "I want the covers," I said. The cold was unpleasant. Why was it so cold in the summertime?

She took out the thermometer and left the room, reading it as she went. "Karl," she said, and I heard her footsteps quick on the stairs.

I slept then, and in my sleep I saw a tall nun standing over me, looking down with her hands on her hips. I could not see inside her wimple, except to notice her glittering eyes.

I woke up when Dr. Kaliski put his hideously cold stethoscope on my chest. Then he took my wrist and counted my pulse. He was a short, bald man who talked through his nose. He asked me if anything in particular hurt. I said that everything hurt. Then he went out, and soon I could hear hammering, but it was very faint.

I began to drowse. After a while, I noticed it had become shadowy. Evening had fallen—but how? Hadn't it been morning just a few minutes ago?

There were wet pillowcases full of crunchy ice all around me and I was absolutely freezing, but too weak to do anything more than moan. I started to feel as if I were flying. Off in the distance, I could hear the ticking again, and I opened my eyes to be sure that I had not accidentally gone back to Mars. My lips hurt, and when I stretched them I felt them crack. Then Candy woke up and began growling at something outside the window.

I knew that I should be afraid to look, that I ought not look. But I did look, and I saw something I don't think anybody is meant to see, something from a world we have left behind us. It was a monstrosity made up of thousands of tiny triangles, triangles around its eyes that made it seem prickly, triangle hair that added an impression of surprise, and gleaming triangle teeth that looked like they could surely bite. It was staring at me through the soft evening light. I felt that it wanted me to die, that it wanted to

63

steal me, that it was waiting like a tiger in tall grass. But there was also in it a strange feeling of appropriateness, as if its glaring evil somehow belonged as much to the order of the world as my mother and father—as if it, also, belonged to God.

The thing of points and triangles seemed to flow with my attention, moving as my eyes moved, going down farther and farther until I had to lean out the window to see it. I knew that this thing was somehow connected with everything that had been happening to me, and I thought that it was the strangest-looking spaceman I had ever seen. There were thousands of dark golden beads in the triangles. It was grinning, had flat black eyes, and looked alive, but I could not believe that anything so strange could possibly be alive. I was scared of it but also fascinated. I watched it slip down past the edge of the window and disappear into the flat roof of the porch below. "Oh, no," I whispered, thinking that it had gone into the downstairs after my family, but nobody raised an alarm and I had to settle back anyway because I was unable to get enough breath and my heart was thumping.

Outside in the yard, some kid sang, "There's a long, long trail a-winding to the land of my dreams . . ."

I could not remember anything that had happened all day. I'd been flat on my back covered with pillowcases full of crushed ice. My breath felt hot against my lips and the ice was starting to seem like fire. I knew that the fever was going up. They knew it, too. Downstairs, they were hammering more ice off the block they'd bought for me.

I was totally, completely exhausted. I felt as if my body was melting into the bed. When I closed my eyes, I whirled slowly around. The hammering became devils beating drums. I did not feel real anymore. I did not feel like I was here.

"It's a hundred and seven now, Mary."

I heard my mother weeping, which sounded very strange, like somebody ripping Kleenex out of a box. Dr. Kaliski, who was shorter than she was, put his arms around her and patted her back. Mother had lost three babies.

I decided that I must be dying. I tried to tell her I was sorry, but I could not form words. I didn't want to die, I didn't want her to lose her best friend, as that is what I considered myself.

Then I was opening my eyes again, and my dad was bathing me with cold washcloths.

That night, somebody came whom I have never forgotten, and whom I am sure I will one day meet again. He was wearing a white T-shirt, and on the right breast there was an insignia that looked like the triangles creature that had been at the window. "My name is Eddie," he said. "I'm here to carry you out."

"You can't carry me, you're just a kid."

"When you're dead."

"I don't want that!"

"If you die now, I'll be your daddy."

I certainly did not want this much younger boy bossing me around. Then he started rubbing my head, and his touch was nice and I felt less dislike for him. So I began to consider dying. "What's it like?"

Eddie cradled me with one arm under my knees and the other behind my neck. It felt weird, as if he was lifting me out of my body. At the time, this didn't seem unusual at all. After a moment, he laughed a little. "Your heart is strong," he said, shaking his head. With a gentleness that was very great, he said, "Not now." He didn't seem totally physical to me, but he was not a ghost. I couldn't quite understand what he was. He was solid, but also kind of translucent. "Maybe later tonight," he said.

I wanted to know who he was. "What's your last name, anyway?"

"Oh, Death."

"Can I tell my momma and dad and sister good-bye first?"

"You better do it soon."

I felt tears on my cheeks.

"Don't be scared of me," he said. "I'm just a kid littler than you are."

"I don't think so."

He gave me a big smile, and I could not help but like this kid. We could have lots of fun together, I could sense that. We could explore Lost Land, or get on our bikes and go out to the freight car remount and eat sandwiches beside the railroad tracks where San Antonio ended and wide-open Texas began. I reached up and tousled his black hair. He did the same to me. He did it a little harder, though, so I did it back just as hard. Then he grabbed my ears and pulled them. I took his cheeks between my forefingers and thumbs and made his lips tight. We were all of a sudden tangled up together, wrestling.

We wrestled on the bed and he was really strong. "No fair," I said, "I'm sick." He got me in a scissors-lock and squeezed until I yelled for mercy. Then I got him in a headlock until he howled. When I finally let him go, his face was red.

Then my mother and grandmother are there looking down at me.

Death leaps at me with his hands like claws. His nails dig into my face and I can feel red-hot scratches going down my cheeks. I grab his throat and choke him as hard as I can. I choke him until his tongue pops out between his pearly teeth and his eyes glare like a puppet's. He wiggles and shakes and twists and then he's free. He gets me around the waist with one arm and gives me a terrific spank with his free hand. It is so hard that I feel like I've exploded. Another one and I see stars. We twist and battle, Death and me, fighting in the moonlight that spreads across the floor.

Then he is not hitting me, he's hugging me, and I know that it's because he has done something I do, which is to scare yourself with your own anger. I stand up in the middle of my bed and the two of us slow-dance to our own music. His head is resting against my chest, and I can smell the warm smell of his hair, like damp straw.

Somewhere far away a woman is crying, almost gagging with her tears. "Mother, he's delirious!"

Granny murmurs, but I cannot tell what she says.

Death is all of a sudden made of dry leaves. He rustles in my arms, and when I jump away he falls apart, crinkling and sifting to the floor, nothing left of him but dust. His voice is still there, though, and he says, "Please be my friend."

"I'll be your friend."

"Forever?"

"Forever and ever."

"You won't fight me when I come back? We'll play? We'll dance?"

It is afternoon and the shades are drawn. Yellow light fills the room. In the yellow light, Father Doiseaux stands with his head bowed. He is wearing his black suit and has a purple stole around his neck. I can hear him praying in Latin, but I can't make out the words. "*In tempora mortis . . .*" "In time of death . . ."

"Are you giving me extreme unction, Father?"

"Yes, I am, Whitty."

Gratitude pours through my veins like healthy new blood. "I thought you'd never get here."

"You'll be with our Lord soon," he says. Like Death, he puts his lips next to my ear. "You just go right up to heaven and Saint Peter will let you in."

"I've sinned."

"Can you say your confession?"

"Bless me, Father, for I have sinned. I buried Patricia's allowance in the rock wall. I crushed Mike's toy stagecoach he got punished for breaking. I took apart the chair my daddy collapsed in and hurt his back. I scared Candy six times with my cap gun. I shot David in a firing squad. I stole the matches Momma thought Annie stole. I put the Elmer's glue in Roxy's mother's shampoo that made her hair get hard."

There, that was done. So it was time at last to sleep. This time Father Doiseaux became Death: he got littler and littler until his priest clothes were in a heap around him and he was just in underpants. "Okay," Death said.

"Okay?"

"Now you go straight to Saint Peter and tell him your name. Then they will open the gates for you, my dear."

On the farthest distance beyond the end of the world, I saw the gates all shining in light and the golden staircase and Saint Peter there on guard. His face was old and deeply etched with caring. He wore a dark blue uniform and a baseball cap, and had a huge book like the book I'd seen on Mars. He looked like about the kindest man in the world. "This is the gate into life," he said. "Are you ready to be born?"

"I thought this was death's door."

"There is no death. You are born into a higher life."

"Where? On the roof?"

That response caused him to fade to a shadow that felt like a memory. Looking around me, I saw that my room was now dark and Candy was asleep at my feet. It felt as if there were bands of dry flesh constricting my throat, and my sinuses were raw inside.

Then Death was back, this time beside the bed. But he couldn't stay there. He seemed to slip and slide away from me. Then he was in the middle of the room, looking down on me with terrible eyes. Then he was against the far wall, his eyes glittering with tears.

Finally he waved good-bye—at which point the fever ended.

COMMENTARY ON THE FOURTH LESSON

The Shaman's Journey

The battle with death is among the most powerful memories of my childhood. It came during a week of profound sickness, but it was not the first time that I had been near death. These fevers had come upon me at regular intervals from the age of about three. My temperature would rise to a dangerous level, my heart rate would become erratic, and the doctor would begin to fear that I had some sort of pneumonia that he might not be able to control.

When I was seven, my immune system had shut down for six weeks after what I remember as a night when a helicopter landed on the flat roof of the porch under my bedroom window.

Since I discovered, from my own experience and those of other witnesses who have met the visitors at my cabin, that being close to the visitors can trigger powerful allergic reactions, I have wondered if these sicknesses did not reflect the physical stress of unremembered encounters.

In any case, I survived the fever. However, this particular battle with death was a very powerful one, and it changed me profoundly. The figure of death became part of me, as things do in childhood, absorbed into the meaning of one's being. Years later, when Amanda Walker, the main character in my novel *Catmagic*, dies and enters the world of the dead, it was the flavor of this experience that I drew upon to lend immediacy to my story.

In all human mystery traditions, the journey through death has been the essential movement that frees the soul to see into other realms. No matter how primitive or sophisticated the religion, it will contain some version of this journey, which in the very earliest times involved a movement both through time and into the stars.

In Christianity, it is commemorated by the liturgical season that runs from Christmas to Easter, as the birth, life, death, and rebirth of Christ are remembered and celebrated. The essential death and rebirth theme is addressed daily in the Eucharist.

The idea of death and resurrection pre-dates Christianity. The first such event was the death of the Egyptian god Osiris and his resurrection by his sister Isis. This evolved into the idea that royal persons could follow Osiris into the stars and immortality. It was the genius of Christianity to proclaim that even the soul of the common man was potentially immortal.

However, the earliest journeys into death did not concern the acquisition of immortality. They were about breaking down the barriers that conceal the world of the dead from living man. Often, shamanic initiations were dangerous affairs that involved extraordinary ordeals, even such basic challenges to death as jumping off a cliff, on the theory that the candidate who was truly chosen would survive the fall.

This journey became reexpressed in many ancient religions besides the Egyptian. It was exemplified, for example, in Greek mythology by the death ride of the god Orpheus and his return to the world of the living. The essential rite of Orphic initiation was called the descent into Hell. This was a more sophisticated version of the early dying god myths, which were in turn elaborations of the basic shamanic initiation.

Because they promised the initiate resurrection, Orphism and the religion of Osiris and Isis were the chief competitors of Christianity during the time of the Roman Empire. The symbolic death of the initiate led to a rebirth into a new kind of life, where the bondage of the ego was broken. The initiate was told, "Ascend beyond all height, descend beyond all depth . . . imagining that you are at one and the same moment everywhere . . . that you have not yet been born, that you are beyond death."

After Christianity gained ascendancy over the old initiatory religions, Western man lost direct access to the old shamanic journey. In the latter part of the twentieth century, however, something has changed this. Although something like the near-death experiences were occasionally reported during earlier periods, it was not until after 1950 that numbers of people in the throes of death began to spontaneously remember the journey that had been intentionally induced in earlier times as an initiatory experience. This may in part be due to the fact that people are more often resuscitated now, and are thus being drawn back from deeper states.

People come back from near-death experiences reporting journeys into other levels of reality inhabited by vividly alive entities that correspond to the spirits reported in the distant past.

Like close-encounter witnesses, they are profoundly shocked by their experiences. As happened to me in childhood, they become unbound in time. Dannion Brinkley, author of *Saved by the Light* and other books about his own near-death experiences, has reported journeys through time similar to mine, as if the shock released him, also, from the grip of the moment. Specifically, Brinkley recounts a journey back to the late nineteenth century while standing near the Tower of London. To him, it also appeared entirely physical.

As a child, I understood nothing of what was happening to me, but the structure was there and it could not have been more clear: from the moment I first dreamed of Mars and began to lose sleep, I had been physically weakened. Then, on the night of the storm, when I not only experienced a severe shock but got soaked through, I was left completely exhausted.

This led to the first great crisis of my life in the secret school, the journey on the wings of fever. In later years, my mother and father told me that I had nearly died that summer. It had happened before, but never so suddenly and never with that intensity. My temperature had remained above 107 for so long that I was probably lucky to escape without brain damage.

Over the next week, I recovered, but not as quickly as might have been expected. I can remember going out in the early morning and looking in newfound wonder at the leaves, the trees, and the sunlight as it poured through the world.

The battle with death had changed me. I was no longer quite as fearful as I had been before. In a deep way, death had become a friend.

My thoughts turned again to the heavens. That drew me back to the ticking of the clock, and very shortly after, to the need to get to that telescope. I had to find a way to attend Mrs. Carter's astronomy classes. The other boys had been going for over a week. I was eager to see the planets, colliding galaxies, and—above all—Mars.

The Wall of Fear

THIS TIME, I ENCOUNTERED A BARRIER THAT SEEMED impossible to surmount. My parents devastated me with the news that I must be in isolation for at least two weeks and maybe the whole summer. I begged them, but they were afraid. There was polio in town, and polio was the terror of our parents' lives.

I did not know where I was on my quest, only that I was being thwarted in something that was terribly important to me. And I was helpless.

When dejected, I liked to spend time in my "office," a nest of branches in the top of the elm tree that overspread our driveway. Day after day, I waited. When Dr. Kaliski arrived in the afternoons about three, I would go down. He would weigh me, poke me, listen to my heart, and then confer hurriedly with my mother. The verdict never changed: better keep him home for a few more days. As soon as it was pronounced, I would rush back up and listen to the shouts and splashes from the pools across the street. I didn't even think about the country club because it made me too sad.

I thought about the telescope, though. I thought about it constantly. When I realized that July was ending, and with it the astronomy class, I began to get desperate. I invented a special germ helmet made out of ammonia-soaked cardboard that I guaranteed would keep me from getting polio. Mother and Dad refused to place any reliance on it.

I heard the ticking of the clock, ticking in the breeze, ticking in my memory and my heart. I peered into the blue and imagined that I could see through the sky's depths to space, to Mars. I remembered the Martian sky like an eye filled with stars.

From my tree, I could hear Mike calling our call, my other neighbor Bill answering. Then my sister would go down the driveway on her bike. As she glided past under the tree, I would drop bark, which generally missed.

I had never encountered anything in my life that seemed as important as that telescope—although, by this time, I had no conscious memory of why I thought it so. I was now acting on two levels, and on the surface some of my behavior would begin to be very strange. It is this automatic behavior, the riding of my bicycle through the night, that eventually remained as the only conscious memory of these events.

An afternoon came when I could no longer bear the waiting. At that point I made what was, up until then, the largest decision of my life. I decided that I would strike out and go to Mrs. Carter's house by myself. Because of the telescope, I knew that I'd have to go at night. To avoid being brought back home by the bus driver, I'd have to ride my bike.

This was a critical moment, perhaps the critical moment of a life that has been devoted to the secret school ever since. The instant I stepped out that door, everything would change for me, and forever. I was on my way to the telescope and a world beyond it that I could not possibly imagine—indeed, that it has taken me most of my life even to begin to understand.

The trouble was that Mrs. Carter lived on Third Street, which was miles away from my house. It was an awful long bike ride. I wished that I could steal one of our cars, but my legs, as I was well aware, were too short to reach the pedals. There was no question about it, though: I had to do this.

The thought of the dark that would be involved was like a vision of drowning. And what if I got caught, what would happen to me then? I had never committed so serious a crime, and had no idea how I might be punished.

I waited through that day in my high places—in the tree, on the roof—entertaining myself with the march of ships and beasts that never ceased to cross my childhood sky. Adults called them clouds; I had concluded that they were the memories of God. The legends of history passed, and dinosaurs, and every clown and troll ever created; the towers of heaven and the mischief of all the storms in the world.

Eventually, I was called down to dinner. Worrying that my mother might somehow read my mind, I ate my supper as if on a stage. I remember nothing of the meal, only that it was at one with the order of those days, with our maid Annie cooking and serving, then the blessing said, and quiet conversation while we ate.

Dinner over, we went into the den to watch TV. We kids had little to say about what was chosen, although we knew exactly what was on and were free to make suggestions. I said nothing, though. I was hardly aware of the TV, and sat through the evening staring at programs like *Beulah, Ozzie and Harriet,* and probably some spy shows without really seeing anything. Feeling like a spy myself and wishing I could take one of Daddy's fedoras to keep down over my eyes like Brian Donleavy, I went upstairs early.

Although it was just to meet and creep about the neighborhood in the dark, we sneaked out fairly frequently, so there was a regular drill for it. The thing was, we did it in groups. This was different. When you were alone, the night was not the same.

When Candy and I were settled, Mom came in and I said my prayers. So I wouldn't fall asleep, I read for about an hour, a book by Charles Beebe about his adventures with the bathysphere in which he had explored the depths of the ocean. I practiced saying the word "abyssal" in the lowest tone possible.

At ten I heard a familiar voice on the TV downstairs, local broadcaster Henry Guerra reading the news on WOAI. I knew that Mother and Dad would shortly come up to check on us for a last time.

Soon, the door opened. I knew to breathe steadily, to be as motionless as possible, not to let my eyelids flicker. My mother had many ways of detecting false sleep. Her best technique in the past had been to snort like a rooting piglet. If she saw the least flicker of a smile, I was caught.

Tonight, though, I must have made her more than usually suspicious, because she used a powerful new strategy. What she did was to growl, low and sinister. It was as scary as it could be, and made me desperate to open my eyes. I fought the fear, fought it with all the strength I possessed. Eventually, she left the room. Now the problem was whether or not she was waiting at the door, silently aware that I had been faking.

The established technique at this point was to delay until you heard the click of the light switch in the downstairs hall. I waited past that, waited until I heard taps echoing across the night from Fort Sam Houston, the army post just to the south of our neighborhood. I said a prayer for the wounded soldiers in Brooke General Hospital, which we always did when we heard taps.

Stealthy childhood sleep overtook me unawares. I didn't even notice it when my eyes closed. I woke up suddenly—aroused, perhaps, by a flicker of awareness that something was going wrong. I sat up in bed. The moon shadows were long. After a moment's confusion, I realized that I'd been asleep for hours. Candy, sensing that I was about to commit a crime, nipped me.

I had to be extremely quiet, because the least little strange noise on the intercom would bring Dad up from my parents' room to investigate.

"I'm coming," I whispered to the night—and thus made the commitment that has defined my life.

I went to my front window and peered out. As

always in the moonlight, the mockingbird that lived in our front yard ran through his repertoire of songs, the cowbird song, the warbler song, even the chirping of our canary.

The night air was filled with scents—the thick perfumes of oleander and huisache and honeysuckle, the lighter odor of the gardenia bushes that grew beside the kitchen walk, the fragile atmosphere of the night-blooming laurel.

I remember those scents with such clarity, and the sound of the trees tossing in the night wind. I remember looking down at the silver moonlight on the grass and the crooked shadows of the trees. How sweet was the air of the night.

I put on shorts and a T-shirt, then gave Candy a precious bit of Snicker's bar to keep her from yapping at me as I left.

Outside, the night flowed like velvet. I crossed the flat porch roof and climbed down the chinaberry tree at the corner of the house. Silence was absolutely critical here. Annie's room was just below, and she knew exactly what it sounded like when a careless boy shook this tree.

I got as far as the driveway before I decided that this was all completely crazy and totally impossible. There was music playing softly in Annie's room, and somehow its faintness made the night seem even bigger. I decided to turn back. There were probably Martian vampires all around here, anyway.

Such a feeling overcame me then as I had never known, a determination so deep that it was beyond even the least hint of denial. I went into the storeroom where our bikes were kept. We had Dunelt

English racers. In our world, this was the bike most prized, and our dad would not have given us less. Mine was blue and it could go like the wind. I was terribly proud of it. I got it out and got on, balancing with my foot as I looked down the driveway.

The image of the dark asphalt strip glowing in the late moon remains vivid in memory even after all these years. A hundred other memories of riding through that dark neighborhood begin with the same image. And now, at last, it was time to go behind the darkness. I had graduated into the night.

I was so scared that I felt physically cold. Nevertheless, I rode off into a dark that would ordinarily have defeated me. By riding as fast as I could, I negotiated the awful blackness beneath the hedge that overarched the driveway entrance. Then I was out in Elizabeth Road, surrounded by the Texas night. My bike had no light, but I didn't need one to see, not with the moon out. I rode up the center of the familiar street, keeping as far from trees and bushes as possible.

I pumped slowly up the hill, passing Nadine Street. Despite the massed vampires at my back and the restless tossing of the trees, I did not break into a panic. It was fascinating to pass my friends' houses, to see them dark, to sense the intimacy of this silence.

I went down the curving two miles to Broadway, which was lighted, although nowhere near as brightly as today. I headed for the center of town. In those days in San Antonio, there was almost no activity after midnight. Virtually the only sound was the mechanism of the streetlights as they blinked on and off. No doubt any passing police car would have stopped me and ended my adventure then and there, but I did not encounter one.

It was a much longer ride than I'd thought it would be, and as I passed the brick buildings of Incarnate Word College on my right, it felt as if I had entered another country altogether.

On I went, past the museum and the public golf course, past Breckenridge Park and Kiddieland, where I had spent so many happy hours. By the time I arrived at Third Street, I might as well have been in Madagascar, as far as I was concerned. I was breathing hard, shaking, hungry and thirsty, but also happy, so very happy that I had actually come this far.

I crossed the San Antonio River on the Third Street bridge. And there it was, ahead and to the right, an enormous old house looking dreadfully haunted. I stopped, staring up at its fortress of tall trees. Above them, far, far up, I saw the gleaming silver of a dome.

How wonderful it looked, how very wonderful, floating there above the treetops, a real observatory. And then it was gone. Total darkness had descended, the dark of a blind man's eye. Then I realized that the moon had just set. I went on more slowly, hardly even able to see the street.

My young eyes got used to the dark quickly, though, and I was soon creeping up to the back porch. It was an old Texas mansion, with big porches upstairs and down and tall windows. It was made of limestone blocks and had a carriage entrance. I went up to the door, opened it, and peered in. It was awful dark in there. The air smelled of beeswax. It was real quiet.

Most people in San Antonio in those days did not lock their doors, and Mrs. Carter certainly wasn't the type to do such an inhospitable thing. People were in the habit of going into their friends' homes without knocking, just shouting "hello" or "woo-hoo" if they didn't see anybody around. It never crossed my mind that there might have been any serious impediment to entering a house in the middle of the night.

As soon as I got in, I could tell that this was a wonderful place. I was aware of the soaring height of the ceilings and all the beautiful woodwork everywhere. Our house wasn't nearly this fancy.

Carefully, I moved forward, wishing that I dared turn on a light. I had to virtually feel my way, and I assumed that Mrs. Carter would have all sorts of delicate things out on display.

I moved slowly down the hallway, toward the glowing patch of light that was the front door. Off to my left, I saw a tiny circular alcove and was fascinated to see that there was a harp in it. I went in and ran my hands along the strings, bringing up just the slightest thrumming sound.

I felt as if I could hear the house breathing. I felt that Mrs. Carter and all of her ghosts were gathering in the dark around me, ready to accuse, pounce, and punish. Still, though, the place was like a magical castle. Opposite the alcove with the harp was a small peaked door. I had noticed it because it was a bit open, and dim light shone from within.

I approached, peered around it. I could see an altar with a candle on it, and some chairs. I wondered if she had a live-in priest. I went in, and coming into the light was like coming in out of the cold. I knelt on the floor and said the Confetior: "O my God, I am heartily sorry for having offended thee . . ." The light of the candle seemed to capture me and make it impossible to leave the chapel. It had ruined my night vision and I was now surrounded by absolute dark, and the dark was alive. I heard breathing sounds and creaks and whispers. I felt the presence of people all around me in the room, and I decided that the house was choked with hundreds of ghosts and I could see their snaky arms and their long, bloody fingernails coming toward me.

I huddled at the foot of the altar, praying for strength and courage in my hour of need, whispering the Litany of the Blessed Virgin. My prayers worked: I gained the courage to rise from my crouch, to come to my feet. But what would I do now—run? I wanted to. I wanted to get back on my bike and go home and put an end to this crazy night. But I was too close to the telescope to give up. It was just a few feet away now, and I sure had come a long way through the dark to reach it.

I went out into the hallway and hid my eyes until I could see again. I'd never go back in the chapel, the chapel was a trap made of candlelight.

I looked up the stairs, which were hideously dark, darker than any stairs I had ever seen. The telescope was way up on the roof, and all the people must be sleeping on the next floor. Did Mrs. Carter live alone? What about the man who had been driving her car at the Witte? Was he in here somewhere? If he found me, he might shoot me or get me sent to Southton, the state reformatory.

This was bad enough to get me sent to Southton,

and maybe I would never see Mom and Dad again. Or what if they woke up and I was gone and they got scared? Tears came to my eyes at the thought of my parents being scared because of me. I had done many crazy things in my life—I was known for this—but this certainly was the craziest.

The back stairs were too dark to use, but there was more light in the front of the house, and I went up the great staircase. At the top of the stairs, there was a rhythmic rattling sound that I thought might be a snake hiding in some dark nook.

For a long time, I just listened, trying to understand where it was coming from and how big the snake might be. Then she sighed, and I understood that it was her breathing. She was *right there*, it turned out, just a few steps away in her bedroom. I peeked in. There were clotted shadows on the bed. On the wall behind it I could see a painting that looked like a landscape. I loved landscapes, and wished that I could see it in the light.

Soon I found another staircase, one that afforded access to the higher parts of the house. I went up, but stopped because it creaked too much. I took off my Keds and went farther, doing the moccasin-stalk that our yardman Fred Ulrich had taught me. Fred had been a cowboy, but had become a yardman because he had been "stove in," as they used to say, by too many range accidents. Fred also taught me how to find water in the desert, how to tell north day and night, clouds or not, how to fish like an Indian with just a little knotted line, and how to fill and roll a cigarette with one hand. He did not, however, teach me how to stop tears of fright from blurring my eyes.

Then I came out into an open space. I guessed that it must be a big attic. It was empty and the floor was wonderfully slick. I just had to run and slide a couple of times. I slid and swayed, then waltzed to what I used to call head music, which was what I heard in my mind. I waltzed with Christina Perez, who was my girlfriend and the love of my life. As I waltzed, I whispered, "My wild Irish rose, freshest bloom of summer," and my fears swept along behind me.

I danced and danced, twirling in the dark, my arms out, my voice whispering and humming, all caution forgotten the instant I had found this wonderful floor. Then I crashed into the wall. The sound of the Empire State Building toppling over would have been a third as loud, if that.

Impulse took over, and before I could stop myself, I yelled, "Excuse me!" Then I clapped my hands over my mouth. How incredibly stupid, how could I get so carried away! I went groping off after the stairs, thinking to make my escape. But I found, instead, a narrow flight that went up.

A pure instinct caused me to go blundering up the stairs. I hit a closed trapdoor and almost fell back, but then found the latch and pushed it open.

All of a sudden I was under the wide, starry sky. I looked up, amazed at how bright and clear it was at this hour. It seemed as if I was on a raft in the middle of space. I looked around for a place to hide. There was only the observatory, surrounded by a low wooden balustrade. I could see steep slate roofs falling off into the dark below.

I went into the observatory and closed the door.

Then I realized that the darned thing was full of windows and was a poor hiding place. For some time, I stayed still, crouching beside one of the windows. But nobody came up through the trapdoor. Nothing stirred but the night wind.

Finally, I turned around. To my nine-year-old eyes the telescope appeared enormous, a great gleaming brass tube pointed at the night sky, a thing from the realm of light-years. The dome was closed, though, so how was I to see? Worse, the machinery to work it was on the outside.

I went back out. There were pulleys and weights and things. I pulled, but there was a terrific clattering sound, so I stopped. I tested the mechanism, and found out that it worked on a counterweight system. When I did it right, the dome opened without a sound. Inside, it proved easy to turn. The movement it ran on was carefully greased. All that was needed was to shove it with a lever.

At this point, the memory becomes more odd, because I no longer recall that I was alone in the observatory ... and I don't remember Mrs. Carter being there, either.

I went on an incredible tour of the heavens that night, but it was no ordinary telescopic adventure. I can remember when I got what I thought was Mars in the scope. Of course, it could as easily have been Betelgeuse, which would also have appeared as a red dot.

The object, as I watched, first shimmered and danced in the scope. I thought that I could see a polar cap, maybe canals. In those days, many scientists assumed that the great Percival Lowell's observations of them meant that they were real. I didn't see them, though, and as hard as I looked, I couldn't find the Sphinx, either. I tried looking out of the corner of my eye, but even that didn't help. Still, this was a scintillating moment. My dreams had come out of my head and into the real world: I had reached the telescope all by myself in the middle of the night, and I was able to see Mars. "It's magic," I whispered.

"Yes," a voice said in the dark, "it is."

COMMENTARY ON THE FIFTH LESSON

Escape

To escape from the slavery of fear, I feel, is to enter real life. And reality, it would appear, is very different from our ordinary and accepted view of the world. But how can we do this? It feels as if we're chained to reality as we know it, that we cannot move an inch, that we cannot hope to change a thing.

The reason that I got to the telescope was that I overcame enough of my fear to take my first nighttime bicycle ride. A nine-year-old is a little slip of a thing, very parent-dependent, only barely capable of self-initiated action. So reaching that telescope was undoubtedly a major test. Had I not passed it, the secret school for me would probably have ended. But after that night I felt different—wonderfully confident and poised and ready for battle.

This was a childhood parallel to the moment that I decided, as an adult, to go into the dark and confront the visitors rather than hide. This process of turning toward the unknown is absolutely essential if progress is to be made. In my case, what I did was discover that my fear could become a form of entertainment. It was desperately frightening to ride that bike through those dark streets, but it was also so thrilling that it seemed to sensitize me to the world in a completely new way, to wake me up, to make me feel, for the first time, entirely alive.

Of course, we want to avoid fear, and my adult life has continued to involve an enormous struggle with it. We tell ourselves that the visitors are evil and to be hated, that we are justified in not trying to understand. Conversely, we call them saviors, which is equally an illusion. In any case, we tell ourselves that we know what they are; we make them concrete as aliens and even give them names. About all we really know is that something very different from us—or that wishes to appear that way—is hiding in the shadows of the night and the depths of the mind.

How very remarkable and mysterious that is, how beautiful. Why should it also be so terrible, and so *unwanted*? Whatever this presence may be, its existence is close to the deepest of human meanings. It can best be defined in the broadest possible way: it is whatever lies behind all the ghosts, demons, spirits, elves, and aliens that we see.

It is not something that can be explained by current theories of reality and the brain/mind, not without ignoring the existence of things like hundreds of hours of incontrovertibly authentic video that have been taken of apparent UFOs since 1991, first in Mexico and then around the world. Neither is it explained by the mythology that surrounds it, old or new.

All of the themes of my life—my fascination with Egypt and Rome and the ancient world, my interest in mysteries and the unknown, my willingness to entertain the improbable, my concern about our environment and our welfare—flow from my time under the shadowy wing of the secret school. So also does the willingness to tempt the unknown. Hidden, always, in the depths of my mind was surely the memory of what I had found behind the darkness, which was a land of wonders.

I do not mean in any way to suggest that fear ought to be suppressed, or that the dark isn't dangerous, or that there is not more than a little of the fool in anyone who tempts the shadow. Without the terror, though, none of the rewards would come. There would be none of the sweetness, not to say the glory, of victory. The marvelous state in which I now find myself, filled as it is with moments of stunning consciousness and softest emotion, would not be available to me.

So on this level, then, fear is actually grace in another dress. The terrible angels of the Bible and the fearsome demons of Tibetan Buddhism are explained, and the fierce love of the dreadful goddess Kali takes on a new meaning. So also does Christ's admonition to love one's enemy. There is an extraordinary benefit: the air after a battle won is sweet indeed.

Unless one builds a relationship with the negative, one cannot gain anything useful from the positive. When we successfully ride the storm, its winds howl the truth and its lightning strikes us with insight.

I am not alone in being thrown onto the saddle of the storm. One of the few consistencies that has ever been found among close-encounter witnesses is the report of great childhood disaster that seems to color so many of their lives. By disaster, I mean an over-turning catastrophe such as the death of both parents or waking up to find oneself being raped by an older sibling or seeing a loved one murdered.

Dr. Kenneth Ring did one of the very few studies of close-encounter witnesses for his book *The Omega Project*. The study revealed that significantly more close-encounter witnesses and people reporting near-death experiences have suffered childhood trauma of an abusive nature than people who are simply interested in these phenomena. The questions asked all involved abusive trauma, but I do not think that this is the only kind that sensitizes a person to the unusual.

In my case, it was the rigors of fever and knowing at such a young age that I might be about to die. I have always remembered Eddie Death. He has come beckoning to me more than once since those days.

When I recovered, I went out into the backyard alone and danced where the old barn owl used to come, the owl of so many hidden meanings. I danced where she would stand her vigil. To me, she was another form of the strange, triangular creature I had seen in my fever dream—a ghost that haunted our lives.

I remembered the bike ride, I remembered the tele-scope, I remembered extraordinary things. How I might have described my memories, though, I do not know. No doubt I would have been furtive, denied that I'd sneaked out. Maybe I couldn't even have spoken of it. But one thing is certain: in the days following, I became a very different child, on the surface much more self-sufficient, beneath it less sure than ever before about what to expect from reality. For me, the cosmic egg had been well and truly cracked.

Among other things, I gained a taste for sneaking out by myself. It was much more fun to be alone, with nobody to whisper warnings and nobody to hang back.

The night was mine. In the night, I could do *anything,* and sneaking into houses became something of a bad habit. I concealed the nocturnal side of my life behind an elaborate screen: I pretended to be even more frightened of the dark than the other kids. The only one who wasn't deceived was my mother. She had developed many ways of detecting whether or not I was asleep, although to my knowledge she never actually came into my room when I was gone. My guess is that we would have had quite a chat about something as serious as that, a chat I would have remembered with painful clarity.

Often, I would find myself waking up at two or three in the morning, and when there was enough moonlight, I would go out onto the flat roof under my windows—just to have a look around. Then I would go to the edge of the roof . . . just to see if our maid's lights were out. If they were, I would go down the tree.

It was real dark back there, which made me want to run, and real close to Annie's room, which forced me to be as quiet as a leaf. Going down the driveway was like navigating a river of mystery. It felt like the trees had eyes, and the coons and the possums might tell on me. As I hurried along, my feet tread softly on the still-warm asphalt.

My objective was to get out into the middle of the street . . . just to see if there were any cars. But once I was there, I was free, and the temptation to keep going was far more than I could resist. I would range through the neighborhood like a little ghost. My power was complete, and I was completely intoxicated by it. Nobody knew, not a soul.

Gradually, my trips became more elaborate. I got my mother to dye a cup towel, a pair of shorts, and a T-shirt dark blue for me. I told her that they were to be a uniform, and even wore them during the day a bit, but it was at night that they were put to their intended use as camouflage. Wearing them, I was no more than a pale-faced shadow.

Some of these little trips still stick in my mind. The more I did it, the more risks I took. At first I just moved about in the neighborhood. By the end of the summer I was entering houses.

I used to play with my friends' toys, pet their animals, and in general impose my secret self on their lives. I would play pranks. During the school year, if I found arithmetic homework, I might change ones to fours and sevens. I might pour Tabasco sauce into the orange juice or scatter clothes all over somebody's bedroom.

I was interested in causing confusion and creating inexplicable mysteries that were like the ones by which I lived. I would leave half-eaten snacks in people's kitchens, or put the dining room chairs up on the table.

But there was more to it than mere pranks, more

even than freedom from fear. The battle with death had also freed me, I think, from a bondage that is right at the center of our meaning as human beings, which is the bondage to time.

We're like fish in water, living as we do in time. Drawn into the air, a fish feels physical agony and what psychological terror that it can. A human being, drawn up out of time, sees more than can be borne—not because of the ugliness, but because of the clarity. The future, the present, and the past implode into a single moment of agonizing truth that can neither be endured nor escaped.

As I stood there in that little observatory, I began to see the telescope in a very different way. What was happening, I think, was that I was beginning to rise out of the time stream, to see things as they appear extratemporally. That was why, I believe, the telescope started to look so strange. I was seeing it not as an object confined to a single moment, but exploded through all the time of its existence.

I had no idea what I was seeing, but I do recall that waves of feeling began to pour over me. I did not want to be there anymore. I felt horribly vulnerable, the terror was beginning to capture me.

One of the things we forget as we mature is just how small a child can feel. I have had many experiences as an adult that made me feel powerless before the grandeur of the universe, but standing there in that dark place all alone, with that telescope changing before my eyes into some sort of monstrosity, I felt absolutely powerless and vulnerable and very, very small.

And then there came the voice of the Sister of

Mercy—rich, sibilant, constructed out of night wind and nightmare, more filled with authority than any other voice I had ever heard, more complete, more sure. It drew me finally out of the safe, warm river that is our world into darkness absolute.

The Secret of the Comets

IT WAS DURING THAT NIGHT IN MRS. CARTER'S observatory that I was finally admitted to the secret school. The long weeks of struggle were over. I did not know it, but from the moment I heard that low, resonant voice reply to my whisper, I was a fully matriculated student of its wonders.

This was the moment that the telescope seemed to change. I backed toward the door, away from what now looked like a dark, matted knot of snakes with skin of polished black metal. I felt very trapped up here, aware that the voice had come from somewhere, thinking that it was Mrs. Carter, and that I had woken her up.

My recollection of the transition that followed is vague. One moment I was at the telescope, then I was lifted off my feet—and suddenly I was walking in a line of children, going along a wooded path.

This is the first memory that I have involving the others in my children's circle. I found myself close behind a boy whom I soon realized I knew from school. He was wearing a white T-shirt and he was so hot that I could see sweat soaking his back.

I recall how it felt to become aware that there were other children with me, and how different they seemed from my ordinary friends. They were like a band of brothers and sisters, closer, older, and dearer companions than any I had ever known. A couple of them I knew from my neighborhood and some from my school, but most of them seemed known to me from some other meaning, some deeper level of reality.

There was a sound, then, a buzzing noise, and the air was filled with the smell of electricity. Hands took mine, the hands of other children who had already done this. I was now physically at the secret school. Without really understanding what had happened, I had been moved from Mrs. Carter's house to the group of benches in the Olmos Basin.

What followed was typical of the lessons of the secret school, taught in pictures and seemingly real experiences that were so strange and emotionally overwhelming that they simply did not enter normal memory.

Something was put on my head. It felt like a football helmet, and its presence in the memory suggests the possibility that I was being subjected to what is now seen as an ordinary product of technology. Now, apparently with a virtual reality helmet seated firmly on my head, I began to see some things that were, to a child in 1954, truly incredible.

Light came around me, causing me to look up. I found myself staring at a vast glowing serpent of stars that crossed the night sky with shimmering reds and purples. Compared to this, the Milky Way was a mere vapor trail. But what was it? There was nothing like this in the night sky, not anywhere in the world.

I wondered if this was what it looked like from a planet *inside* a pair of colliding galaxies. I gazed upward, aware that I could be seeing a tremendous engine of destruction, a death zone.

It was so huge and bright and complicated, with blue and red eddies, with vast reefs of glowing gas, that the sky seemed like the dome of a phosphorescent cave. There was a feeling, suddenly, that it was about to fall on me. My breath caught and I turned away. I did not want to look up again. Beautiful it may have been, but I had—and have—never seen anything that appeared remotely as dangerous.

Off to the right was a squat, domed building that reminded me of a concrete pillbox or a small fort. There wasn't a sound or a movement, not a sign of life. Was I really here, I wondered, really on a planet in the colliding galaxies, a place where they knew to the day and hour when their world would end?

The question resonated . . . a world that knew the day and hour of its own ending, the day that they would enter the beautiful zone overhead . . .

I could certainly understand the funereal silence, as well as the strange solidity of the little building. People in a place like this would want strong forts.

The reason that I so quickly understood what I was seeing was that I had already spent many hours wondering about colliding galaxies and what it would be like on a planet in one.

Life would evolve and conscious creatures would come forth and look about and fade away before the deadly wheel turned its fatal turn. They would look up, and in ignorance they would probably call it heaven. But some of them would surely reach a point where they could understand the meaning of the glory, and come to see that their paradise was actually their doom. Would it change them when their astronomers finally calculated the day that they would enter the zone?

The colliding galaxies and the planet silenced by contemplation of its end faded. I was drawn up from that surface and back into the basin. I didn't feel that I was dreaming, but I obviously wasn't having an ordinary experience.

Now I heard the gushing sigh of the night wind. Around me there were dim forms. It became clear to me that I was sitting on a wooden bench. I may have said hello, but I don't remember anybody else saying anything.

A little boy is taken out of his life and made to confront a strange machine. Maybe he resists, maybe he even screams, but he looks in it, he cannot resist, first once and then many times.

He sees a glowing mass of material, pure white. Above it there is a comet, and the comet is moving. I recall the tail, which was very different from that of an ordinary comet. You could see its movement, you could see it luffing like a winded sail.

The comet enters the huge whiteness, which seems to be a gas cloud, and as it does, there is a sudden increase in its brightness. Then, quite rapidly, the interior of the cloud begins to change. Its shape alters into an egg, then an ellipse. There is a sense of titanic work being done, and I am told, or the thought comes to me, that this is the way it looked when our world was beginning.

Very clearly now, I remember that my response was to cry out, and my child's voice, I sense, was joined by the cries of other children. The cries change nothing, though: I am compelled to look.

The ellipse now has a ball at each end, one much larger than the other. They are both encased in a chalky, fierce whiteness. The smaller one is orbiting the larger at what seems a short distance, but I have no sense of scale. This could be something the size of a toy, or the balls could be thousands of miles across.

Then the person who is with me puts her hand on my shoulder. I hear a girl's voice sing sweet and soft: "I see the moon, the moon sees me, high up in the old oak tree."

At that moment, I understand what I am seeing. This is a view of very ancient times. The Earth has been hit by a huge meteor and the moon is breaking off—and then the vision ends.

I find myself sitting on one of the benches. My temples hurt, my mouth is sand-dry, I feel as if I've been twirling round and round to make myself dizzy. I recall that I was given a drink of water, and somebody who looked to me like the Sister of Mercy I had seen in my Mars dream held her hand against my forehead.

"Where am I?" I asked.

"School," she said. Her tone was so matter-of-fact that I thought I was on the grounds of my grade school. I tried to look around me, but before I could see any details, I found myself being lifted to my feet, being brought toward the helmet again.

I understood clearly now that I was no longer at Mrs. Carter's, that we were in the woods somewhere. I struggled, I twisted back and forth. In my ear there came a voice. It was making strange, high-pitched sounds that communicated distress. Holding my arms, the owner of this voice pressed my head once again up into the black orifice.

Around me, other children were singing, "I see the moon, the moon sees me . . ." I remembered being told at some point that we were supposed to sing to calm each other down.

This time there was a sensation of physically shooting right out through the helmet. I dropped a few feet, stumbled into soft, mushy ground. This felt like the ordinary earth. I stood there, too scared to move.

It seemed as if I was in a jungle of some sort from the dampness, the smell of rot, and the warm, wet fronds of things that touched my face. The shadows pulsated with life—screaming, clattering insect life. The place was full of scurrying creatures, some of which seemed larger than rats, their carapaces gleaming in the faint light from above.

They crawled on me, rushed up my legs. I screamed, I pulled them off—and another nightmare was added to my future repertoire. From then on, I would be troubled by the memory of how it felt to have those creatures crawling on me. Many a night, my mother would carry me naked to the bathroom mirror to prove to me that I was not covered with scorpions.

Even as I write this, the sensation returns. Many close-encounter witnesses report a similar horror of insects, especially spiders. I wonder if their fears reflect buried memories similar to mine.

At nine, I had a limited concept of the past. To me, wherever I happened to be was here and the time was always now, which made all this far more terrifying. I did not understand that I had gone, at least figuratively, sweeping back across the reaches of time. I thought that the world had been invaded by giant bugs.

Then a huge moon began rising, a moon so large that there was the illusion that I was looking down at it and would fall to its immense, bleak surface or be impaled on its mountains. These were clearly visible. They looked craggy and brutal.

In the moon's light, large shapes took whirring flight, their wings rattling like New Year's noisemakers. They drew my eyes upward, but I could not see them clearly. The sight of that ancient moon fully risen was awesome indeed. It has been hanging in my memory ever since, glaring with yellow-golden light. It easily filled a quarter of the sky.

The voices of the children continued singing, ". . . high up in the old oak tree," and I heard them as if they were high above me. I felt that I had fallen like Icarus, who was one of my favorite mythological figures.

The moon raced up the sky, going so fast that it

made me feel as if I was moving instead. Trailing it, I saw another object, a silver moonlet, star-shining.

Brushing bugs off me, I put my arms out, attempting to gain some comfort, but there was nobody. This all seemed so real that it was hard to believe that I would ever be anywhere else. I can't remember anything about the fauna and flora, except that the place was abundantly alive. Because of the appalling event that was about to unfold, though, I can surmise that this was intended to be the late Permian, a quarter of a billion years in the past.

The loneliness was horrible. Even if this was some sort of optical illusion, I believed it completely. As far as I was concerned, I was there. Terror grew, it grew into a titanic storm inside me, it burned my soul, it made me twist as if in physical agony, it made me shriek in my high boy's voice.

Just as I was beginning to panic completely and run off in any crazy direction, I found myself drawn up out of the jungle. I didn't have a chance to cry out my relief before I saw that I was floating in the dark of space. The awful helmet was pressing against my head. I ran in the emptiness, my feet treading nothing.

"One day you'll thank me for this," the Sister of Mercy said, her gravelly voice startlingly close to my ear.

I do thank her now, in humility and in awe, for the enormous lesson that came my way that night.

Immediately, I was on a surface, but not the surface of the Earth. There was no loam, there was no jungle. Thankfully, there were no insects.

The sky was most remarkably changed. The moon

was even larger, this time so vast that I felt as if I could step out and walk on it. I reached up, I spoke, hearing the old song again, "I see the moon, the moon sees me . . ."

But if I could see the moon and I wasn't on Earth, where was I? It was a strange little place with very cozy horizons. I seemed to be in a tiny, featureless valley. I glanced up, and when I did, I saw the most appalling thing that I had ever witnessed. Because it was so obviously huge, it was far more terrifying than the comet hitting the gas cloud had been.

What I saw was that the whole firmament was filled by a wall of dark blue. For a moment I did not know what to make of it. I thought that I was in a huge room—but then realized that the "wall" was composed of water, because I could see long, wrinkled lines of waves.

Then I realized that I was also seeing low, green-brown land areas, and understood that I was above a planet. There were no familiar geographic features, but it must have been Earth, because the moon was easily recognizable.

I got the sense that I was falling from a great height. I concluded that I must be on a meteor. I assumed that it was the small silver object I had seen near the moon when I'd looked up. So I had been transported from the surface of the Earth to the surface of a small asteroid that was floating between the Earth and the moon.

Realization blasted through me: the asteroid was crashing, and I was on it. I remember just groaning inside at the idea that a nightmare could turn into an even worse nightmare.

Like so many incidents from that night, the vision of the dark ocean seen from a great height has remained in me ever since, unattached until now to anything outside of itself. Many times I have seen that water in my mind's eye, dark and dangerous in the moonlight.

The planet below began to get much larger. Because of a movie I had seen, *When Worlds Collide*, I was well aware of the meaning of this phenomenon. This was a cosmic collision, just like what was happening on a more massive scale in the colliding galaxies. It was the end of the world, I decided.

I was transfixed by the rapidly approaching ocean surface. It was so real that it was impossible for me to believe that I wasn't about to get smashed to bits. It still hadn't occurred to me that the event I was seeing was eons in the past. I cried out, trying to warn my family to get into the basement. I had to save Candy and my hamsters and our canary. I had to save my mother and father and sister and all my relatives.

Wind began screaming, the rock glowing red, now yellow. I had no feeling of physical sensation, but was pressed back against the stones. The sea spread before me, quickly getting closer. Then everything became white fury.

I was on the bench again. My temples hurt, my chin hurt. "We're adjusting your pilot hat," the Sister of Mercy said.

Then I saw the scene from an outside observer's perspective. Flaring and burning, the asteroid shot downward, then hit with a blistering white glare. An immense shock wave raced out toward the ends of the ocean. Out of the fiery haze at the center something like a giant pillar studded with lightning came gushing up. It began spreading in the moonlight, and I thought that it looked like the biggest Christmas tree in the world.

The planet shuddered, then actually rolled, and the pillar of sparkling fire went off across the horizon. Land came into view—land that was cracking open, revealing fissures that spat molten stone so high that I could see the smoking, rolling boulders as they crested their arcs just below me.

The whole world was rolling like a gigantic ball in the firmament, turning and turning, hopping . . . and throwing off huge pieces of itself that went tumbling outward, went screaming and rushing up out of the mantle of air, briefly leaving gouges full of steam and rocks that oozed like molten plastic, rocks of unimaginable immensity, the raw edges of a tremendous hole into which the sea was pouring like white lace.

I screamed until my throat popped, screamed until I became my screaming, and heard around me equal screaming.

The helmets were impacting our unprepared minds with visions that we took to be actual events. We could not distinguish a vivid multimedia presentation from reality. In 1954 such things were completely unheard of. These ordinary objects—now available in any game store for a few hundred dollars—carried us screaming into the unknown on an electronic raft.

Who could do this in 1954 I do not know. What I do know is that their show was not over. We were struggling to escape, our helmets tossed here and there. Our little bodies squirmed and fought to get away and the place echoed with shrieks as dramas of terror were played out in the brush—a girl racing toward the giant old tree, only to be set upon and dragged back by the scruff of her neck, a boy throwing himself off the edge of the bluff, to be caught and returned to his place on the bench.

For years, I discounted all of this as a series of fever dreams, but I do not think so now, not now that I have discerned the overall structure that was hidden not only within each lesson, but in the whole syllabus of the school. No, I am describing a message that was planted in us, one that contains scientifically valid meaning and might be of extraordinary importance.

The Sister of Mercy addressed me. "Do you want to come back to us?"

"I'd like to go home now, please, Sister," I replied.

She thrust me along from behind, rushing me down a path to where we'd left our bicycles. But . . . hadn't I gone to Mrs. Carter's? Wherever this was, it was out in the middle of the brush.

I looked down, amazed to see my bike here. I remember reaching down, touching the familiar handlebars . . .

Then it was morning, the sky was blue, the mourning doves were cooing in the backyard, and the smell of bacon was wafting up from the kitchen below. I sat up in bed, momentarily disoriented. I'd had a nightmare. I remembered bugs, bugs and meteors. I shuddered.

I noticed that Candy was standing on the foot of the bed, growling out into the sun-flooded bedroom.

When I touched her, she reacted with a snarl, but I comforted her and got her to come into my arms—where she proceeded at once to fall into a deep sleep. She was one exhausted animal.

I put her in her usual place beside my pillow and got up. If I was going to get my share of that bacon, I had to dress fast.

COMMENTARY ON THE SIXTH LESSON

A Theory of Creation

I have no memory of the journey back to my bed after the lesson was over. In that sense, I am obviously dealing with the grammar of dream. But it is hard for me to believe that I could have invented, even in a dream, the virtual reality viewer when I was nine. I have put some of the new video helmets on recently, and I think that the ones available in arcades today are quite similar to what was being used on us then.

It isn't particularly difficult to see the outlines of what might have been very real events. After all, the secret school was physically real; the benches, tree, and other ruins are there.

Hypnosis could have been used to obscure the movement from Mrs. Carter's house to the Olmos Basin. Maybe I was simply taken in a car. The same is true of the trip home. As far as sleep is concerned, I would have been exhausted, so I might have even been asleep before we arrived back at the house.

There is now little that's actually all that mysterious

about what was done. But in 1954 the technology did not even exist to build viewers on a small enough scale to fit in a helmet. Color television was just coming into use. There were no transistors, and miniaturization was in its infancy.

Many witnesses besides myself have written me about helmets being put on their heads. Often, the helmets leave painful marks on their temples, usually triangular in shape. If you wanted to project images into a human brain, the temples, close to the temporal lobes, would be the place to do it. A witness I know well, special effects artist Steve Neill, says that he has "indentations like slices of pie" in his temples that often grow inflamed after his experiences, which are highly visual.

I have often wondered if Neill's vivid paintings of other worlds might not be inspired by his own childhood in the secret school, or even by current lessons.

As advanced as it was at the time, somebody had this equipment in 1954, and even more than the equipment, they had the ability to introduce me, in their theater of dreams, to a view of the past that is just now gaining scientific credibility and was entirely different from what was believed then.

The night began with a vision of colliding galaxies that superficially did not seem related to the series of visions that came after. It was about the final end of a world, while the others all concerned creation. In one sense, it began the lesson with its own end. In another, though, it reminded that creation is a flux, not a flow. It waxes and wanes. One world's dying is the beginning of another.

The more detailed material concerned life on Earth,

and illustrated the fact that the two most critical events in earthly evolution were caused by the impact of huge meteors.

In 1954 accepted scientific theory was that evolution had occurred gradually, and that the key to understanding the origin of species was to find all the "missing links" that connected present forms of life to their extinct forebears. The idea that anything, let alone impact events, might be dramatically disrupting the steady flow of evolution was simply not known. Now, however, more is understood about this process, and we are aware of the importance of sudden environmental change on the evolutionary process.

So a child's dream—or experience—of forty years ago bears a direct relationship to the very latest scientific thinking about the mechanism of evolution— so recent, indeed, that science is just now putting it all together.

For example, I saw something slam into a glowing orb that appeared to me to be the Earth, whereupon it broke into two pieces. We know now that the moon probably did emerge out of the same protomatrix as Earth. Structurally as well, it is similar to Earth. It may even contain an iron core at the base of its asthenosphere, or deepest interior layer, just as Earth does. It is about the same age as the Earth.

Science has, at least in part, recently come to the conclusion that the moon actually formed out of earthly materials that were ejected from the planet by an impact. I could not have known that in 1954. Back then, there were three leading theories about the origin of the moon: that it had been captured, that it had split off from the Earth because the primordial planet was spinning so fast, or that Earth and moon had formed slowly as twins.

These theories remained in vogue until the Apollo moon missions resolved the matter in a surprising way. In 1984 a conference was held on the island of Kona in Hawaii, so that selenologists who had been studying the information from the rocks brought back by the missions could come to a consensus about the moon's origin. One of the organizers, G. Jeffery Taylor, describes the outcome as follows: "By the end of the deliberations, a clear consensus formed in support of the idea that the impact of a large projectile with the growing earth dislodged the material that would form the moon."

That is precisely what I saw in my childhood vision, thirty years before this conclusion was reached by science. But there's more to it than that. I was seeing the moment when life on Earth became possible. Without the slowing effects of the moon's gravity, the planet's thousand-mile-an-hour rotational speed would cause constant surface winds of at least three hundred miles an hour. The gentle winds that characterize our weather would instead be a ceaseless hurricane. Water vapor, borne aloft by the wind, would sheathe the planet in an unending cloud cover. What little life might exist would be in the form of bacteria and small creatures like lichen clinging to rocks. There wouldn't be enough light reaching the oceans for there to be higher evolution there, either.

So it is not the Earth that is the cradle of life, but the Earth-moon system. Life does not depend on a planet, but on a synergy between two planets operating in perfect balance. No planet, it seems, with a profile similar to Earth's could sustain life without an unusually large moon in just the right orbit. I was thus witness to the creation of a mechanism designed to support life—an Earth-moon machine.

With no ability to sample other solar systems in detail, we cannot know how common it is for planets like ours to have large moons. But the need for something to retard rotation-driven winds must severely limit the number of planets on which higher life-forms can evolve.

In fact, the Earth-moon structure is so carefully balanced that it is hard to think of it as the outcome of chance. It looks much more like a construction of some sort—an incubator, if you will—given the exquisite balances that are involved.

The statistical likelihood that an exactly balancing moon would form may be low, but the likelihood that a planet would happen to fall into the narrow livable region around its star may be even lower. However, when it becomes necessary for these two incredibly unlikely events to be combined in order to create an incubator for higher life-forms, then the probabilities virtually vanish. Even a universe ten times the estimated size of our own may not have enough chance in it to account for such a phenomenon.

Added to this must be the fact that, from the experience of our own planet, the universe is a dangerous place. So some of the livable systems that do evolve are bound to be destroyed by the same sort of impacts that started evolution in the first place. With this possibility added into the mix, the odds against conscious life evolving anywhere at all become more than negligible.

In fact, in our universe it would seem that the existence of conscious creatures who are dependent upon an Earth-moon system like ours cannot be accounted for by chance. And yet we exist, and there is strong circumstantial evidence that we not only aren't alone, but that somebody else is here watching—or watching over—us.

John Barrow and Frank Tipler, in their book *The Anthropic Cosmological Principle,* make an argument that the probability of creatures evolving to the point that they gain the capability of interstellar travel is so low that we are likely to be alone in our galaxy. Their argument uses the Drake Equation, which is a measure of the likelihood that such species will develop based on a series of probabilities. The second of these probabilities is an estimate of the number of planets that will be habitable in a given galaxy. The recent realization that the moon is critically important in making Earth habitable has reduced this probability even further. But it's a mixed bag. While the likelihood that conscious creatures will evolve anywhere is virtually nonexistent, the chances that they will eventually *be* everywhere if they do evolve is surprisingly high.

This is because the assumptions behind Drake's Equation that estimate the likelihood of other intelligent creatures reaching here have also changed. *If* they exist, then it is probably inevitable that they will be here sooner or later.

The original equation was derived with the belief

that faster-than-light travel is impossible, and therefore that the colonization of a galaxy would take about a million years. Given that our galaxy is ten billion years old, the thinking went, the fact that they aren't already here means that they either don't exist or cannot maintain social structures over interstellar distances because of the thousands of years it would take for messages to go back and forth.

However, two things have changed since the equation was accepted as a critical rationale against alien contact. The first is, as Ian Crawford of the University College of London says in the Fall 1995 issue of the *Quarterly Journal of the Royal Astronomical Society*, "Contrary to popular belief, faster-than-light speeds are not explicitly forbidden by special relativity. They would, at least in principle, make possible galaxy-wide social and political structures like the *Star Trek* Federation."

Methods of traveling faster than light are now being postulated by scientists. Crawford suggests the use of "wormholes," or shortcuts through space-time such as those described by Kip Thorne and Michael Morris of Caltech. Another possibility, proposed in the June 11, 1995, issue of *New Scientist* by Miguel Alcubierre of the University of Wales in Cardiff, is a "warp drive," which would enable a vehicle to escape the curvature of space, thus rendering distance meaningless.

The vast energies upon which such drives must depend will become available when we begin to be able to control antimatter, which is also a subject of serious scientific speculation.

It would thus appear that, if there is even a single other intelligent species anywhere in the universe and they have developed technology that can transmit them at hyper–light speeds at any time in the past, then they are likely to be here.

So the UFO enigma finally acquires a basis in hypothesis. The light-speed objection inherent in Drake's Equation is gone, which leads to a discussion of the second thing that has changed in recent years. This takes the form of the video evidence, primarily from Mexico and, more recently, Colorado, that has been alluded to earlier in this book.

This new video evidence has in general been taken by casual camcorder users, often in public situations, and is impossible to simply reject out of hand. The fact that it is so often ignored by the media is not a sign of its invalidity, but a symptom of our cultural and emotional bias against the unknown.

For years, the main objection to the presence of aliens in our midst has been the notion that the vastness of interstellar distance makes their coming so improbable. That objection, it would seem, is gone. It now seems that nothing but an emotional commitment to cherished beliefs prevents science from taking an entirely new look at the UFO phenomenon.

Because they generally assume that a casual study of this extremely complex and subtle situation is sufficient, scientists and intellectuals aren't looking deep enough. Now that it is clear that there are travelers here from *somewhere*, and there is ample evidence building in physics that they could originate either in space or time, the tradition of denial should be seriously questioned.

However, there is certainly no evidence that huge hordes of them are here, or even that there is any urgency in the sense that they are about to impose themselves on us in some negative way. To the contrary, the more we know about them, the more useful a closer relationship with them is coming to seem.

It may be that correctly articulating what they are will be among the last things that we do during the long journey into contact. This is because we will need to gain much more experience with life on their extratemporal and physically unbound scale before we can even begin to define them.

Certainly, our present definitions—that they are aliens, "extra-dimensionals" (whatever that is supposed to mean), or that they simply don't exist—are very primitive. For example, even if their original physical matrix is another planet in this universe, what can a concept like "alien" or "visitor" possibly mean to somebody who must view the universe as part of an object with more dimensions than we can conceptually include? If they are outside of time—and a flood of evidence points to this—then where are they? It's no wonder that people see them walking through walls and levitating. That must be the least of it.

It may be that the reason they hang back in the shadows of our culture as they do is that we cannot communicate with them or about them, and will not be able to manage this until we empower ourselves as extratemporal creatures also. The way we are now, we risk, by mere association with them, a descent into nonmeaning very much like that which has destroyed so many of our own world's magic-believing societies when faced with the true magic of Western science. The picayune miracles of quantum physics are no match for a time traveler's *juju*.

Whether it is intentional or not, their physical appearance among us is certainly an extremely rare phenomenon. Could it be that they themselves are extremely rare—as rare as we are?

It is possible to glimpse the actual rarity of mankind by reversing a common statistic: there are over 45,000 gigantic, roaring, bigger-than-you-can-imagine *stars* in our one little galaxy alone . . . for each human creature on this earth.

We are commonplace only to ourselves.

Given the exacting criteria needed to induce a conscious species to emerge in the life of a planet, it is possible to entertain the idea, as Tipler does, that consciousness, quite simply, has no way of happening without intervention. To see what the mechanism of intervention might be, it is necessary to examine the engine of evolution a little further.

The structure of the second vision, which appears to have involved the cataclysm that closed the Permian era many millions of years before the first dinosaur so much as grunted, also fits recent scientific thinking to a compelling degree.

That anything survived the unspeakable hell I witnessed is a miracle. The Earth rolled around on its axis. It burst open, and lava poured out of the side opposite the impact. I cannot express the effect of this memory, although I can certainly see why it was buried in amnesia, with its terrible power and the sense of vulnerability that it conveyed.

Let me draw a picture of the late Permian as science has reconstructed it. Life had existed for about three hundred million years. Mostly, the Earth was covered with water. There were, however, some large landmasses, and living things had come up from the sea about a hundred million years before. The great radiation of species onto dry land that had taken place over that time knows no subsequent parallel, no more than does the absolutely stunning totality with which the Permian world was extinguished.

The close of the Permian took place 245 million years ago. No extinction since has come close to equaling it. For over 300 million years, complex living creatures had been evolving on the Earth, thriving in its broad, warm seas and then upon the shoulders of the land. They spread up from the beaches and the lagoons, a march preceded by primitive plants like the pteridosperms, palm-like relatives of modern ferns. Slowly, as first the Cambrian passed, then the Ordovician, then the Silurian, creatures struggled in the seas until they were teeming. In the Devonian, about 400 million years ago, primitive lagoon-dwelling creatures began to seek space by going into the shallows. Through unimaginable gulfs of time they did this, often getting trapped beneath the sun, often dying. But not always.

By the end of the Devonian, vertebrates were swarming out onto the land, following the plants and the insects. This was followed by the Carboniferous, when the first winged insects and the first reptiles appeared.

Then came the Permian, that most remarkable of eras, for it is among the creatures of the Permian that the great extinction that I saw in my vision would take place, and it is out of the suffering few who survived—a shattered band of reptiles and proto-mammals—that the whole future emerged.

All during the Permian, there was a steady decline of species on Earth. Plankton died back at one point, just as it is doing now, causing food shortages so acute that whole schools of fossil fish are sometimes found from this period, which apparently starved and died together.

Evolution, after all, is both alpha and omega, the beginning and the end. The omega moment for one species is the alpha point for another. Ancient lines bow down to death, new ones take their place.

The close of the Permian was, on a larger scale, similar to the much more recent end of the Cretaceous that destroyed the dinosaurs 65 million years ago. Like the end of the Permian, the end of the dinosaur era took place when a long period of decline was terminated by a violent catastrophe.

In 1994 the beginning of a dieback of plankton was noted off the California coast. As in the Permian, this dieback is occurring during a general decline of species. In our case, the dieback did not start as recently as we assume. It has actually been under way for at least twenty thousand years and probably longer, so belching factories are not the only problem.

Camels, giant ground sloths, and numerous other large mammals disappeared from North America thousands of years ago. Mammoths and mastodons were eradicated across the entire planet by ten thousand B.C. And this was just the beginning. The process has continued without surcease into the present era. By 1995 the decline of species has become dramatic, with whole genuses, such as the amphibians, apparently beginning to come under general threat.

We do not know exactly what caused the long decline that culminated in the Permian catastrophe, but we think that the present environmental decline is due to a mechanism similar in part to the one that we know was under way before the dinosaurs were destroyed. At that time, also, the proliferation of a single species had overburdened the environment. Today, the species playing the role of the dinosaur is us.

Our population explosion has been so aggressive in the past fifty years that the kind of large-scale management that would be necessary to reverse the wholesale extinctions of other species that are taking place all around us is no longer possible. We were unable to develop science that was sufficiently correct or social institutions powerful enough to manage our own growth, so the evolutionary crisis of the present era is going to happen according to the laws of nature, not of man. What might this mean?

Again, the vision comes into play, and the vision, it turns out, is surprisingly suggestive. After the object impacted the ocean, huge fissures opened up on the other side of the planet and white-hot lava spewed out in miles-high geysers.

It turns out that this fits a recently proposed explanation for the massive upwellings of magma that have characterized Earth's geologic history. Lava fields from over a hundred such events have been found, the largest in Siberia and India. When active, these lava fields have given off millions of tons of gases and set massive fires, causing planet-wide devastation and upheaval lasting for thousands of years.

What causes the lava fields? Interestingly, the dream showed a possible process clearly. An astral body hit the planet, delivering a shock so terrific that it bounced on its axis. Then, on the opposite side of the Earth from the impact, lava began gushing out. This obviously suggests that the shock caused the lava to emerge.

Modern science is beginning to corroborate this radical view. In the August 13, 1993, issue of *Science*, a remarkable discovery was detailed by Dr. Asish R. Basu. What he and his colleagues discovered was that these lava fields contain quantities of helium-3, a primordial gas associated with magma from very deep in the Earth. "We are proving definitively that it's from the core-mantle boundary," Dr. Basu said.

The eruption I witnessed was probably the largest of them all, the Siberian basalt flood that took place 245 million years ago and was part of the great evolutionary engine that closed the Permian and almost ended life on Earth altogether. This tremendous eruption sent out enough molten rock to cover the entire surface of the planet to a depth of ten feet. Although the eruption was more localized than that, and there were surface areas left untouched, the destruction was on a scale that is completely unimaginable.

What, then, would cause such an eruption? My dream was clear: it followed the impact. On August 22, 1995, the *New York Times* stated, "Recently, scientists have proposed that a speeding asteroid or comet, colliding with Earth and exploding with the force of millions of hydrogen bombs, might have shot gargantuan shock waves through the globe."

The waves would have concentrated on the opposite side of the planet, causing the crust to shatter. There would have been vast outpourings of lava. The *Times* goes on to say that this theory—antipodal volcanism—is not yet widely accepted, but is intriguing to many scientists as a line of research.

More is known about the end of the dinosaur era, since Luis Alvarez found convincing evidence in 1979 that this particular mass extinction was caused by a cometary impact. The evidence reveals that the Yucatan was the epicenter of the impact, and an area of massive magma outflow on the Indian subcontinent known as the Deccan Traps also dates from the period. Geographically, the lava tide did not occur opposite the Yucatan impact, but it happened at the same general time and may well imply the presence of an as-yet-undiscovered impact elsewhere.

When a tremendous impact takes place, a huge jet of material pours upward into the stratosphere while devastating shock waves radiate out from the target point. This material, consisting of white-hot rock, drops down across a vast area of the planet, setting everything on fire. Added to this are earthquakes, massive lava flows, and possibly polar shifts caused by the planet's gyrations.

In other words, this quiet, stable home of ours, with its clockwork-perfect days and precise seasons, can be completely overturned in an instant, without warning. A given day changes radically and nothing is ever the same again.

Are we looking, here, at a great mechanism of destruction that is also the key to evolution? David Raup of the University of Chicago has identified a

30-million-year cycle in mass extinctions that is apparently associated with an extraterrestrial cause, possibly impact-related. Such a long cycle could even be related to the movement of the solar system around the galaxy, and Mineo Kumazawa of Nagoya University in Japan suggests that the mathematics of chaos may reveal a nonlinear determinism in these seemingly random events that may cause them to play a surprisingly structured evolutionary role.

This sounds impossible, but other research being done by physicists William Ditto, Yuri Braiman, and John F. Lindner, as reported in the November 30, 1995, issue of *Nature*, suggests that introducing random variables into chaotic systems causes them to become organized, rather than more disordered as common sense would tell us that they should. Maybe random impacts smashing into a planet's chaotic evolutionary process actually cause large-scale organization to emerge.

Certainly, on a grand time scale, things look extremely well organized. Life on earth has moved from single-cell organisms to man without a single era during which simpler creatures than those of the era before dominated.

I have wondered, in fact, if the declines themselves may not provide what chaos theorists refer to as a strange attractor, a factor that adds structure to apparently random events. In this sense, the declines and the impacts could be in some arcane way related: the one could attract the other.

In any case, evolution is a very strange process, and its laws are at best poorly understood. For example, why don't the same species that were nearly killed off slowly regenerate in their old forms? Obviously, this is to some extent because their living environment disappears and does not return after the planet becomes stable again. But that is not always the case. It wasn't even the case at the end of the Cretaceous. There were dinosaur species living in all sorts of climates on every landmass on the planet. Some of them were as small as the mammals that survived, and used the same parts of the food chain.

We know what devastated the planet, but not precisely why dinosaurs and only dinosaurs were completely extinguished. It was useful, though, because it left room for species with more potential to evolve.

This suggests another very strange thing about evolution. There is no reason why these catastrophes would lead to evolutionary progress, and yet they always seem to.

At least 97 percent of species were destroyed at the end of the Permian. Chance would have dictated that a mix of primitive creatures would have survived along with the more modern ones, but this is not what happened. In fact, every impact shows the same aftermath: even though they are not necessarily the most robust, the creatures most capable of evolving are the ones that seem to survive.

Edward Teller, the "father of the H-bomb," has suggested developing a system that can deflect or destroy potentially dangerous asteroids because the statistical probabilities favor a major impact, as it has been so long since one has occurred. There is controversy about whether such a system should be built before we gain the capability to survey the hazard, which we cannot now do with any degree of accuracy. In 1998 a

$120 million Pentagon project will launch a satellite, *Clementine 2*, to fly past three asteroids and fire guided missiles at them as a feasibility test.

That such a program would be useful became, in May of 1996, a hard thing to question. On May 19, an asteroid a quarter of a mile in diameter unexpectedly passed within 270,000 miles of Earth. This object, christened 1996 JA-1, was discovered just a short time earlier. It was the largest object recorded passing this close to the Earth, and was one of only five objects known to have passed so close.

Had 1996 JA-1 struck the planet, life would not have been extinguished, but human civilization is unlikely to have survived. There is no reason to dwell on the morbid details of the devastation that would have been involved; suffice it to say that it would have been extraordinary. In the case of this object, had it been aiming for Earth, we would have had only a few days of warning.

Shortly before the discovery of 1996 JA-1, another object was discovered that passed only 1.9 million miles from Earth in late May. Whether or not a defensive perimeter would work, or if such efforts even matter in the larger scale of things, remains to be determined.

In any case, the overall thrust of evolution has always been toward more of what could most appropriately be described as elegance of structure. For the most part, animals tend to end up in forms that simply work better than what came before. But why? Why isn't it just a matter of chance? The whole creation and evolution of life on this planet begins to appear more like the outcome of a design.

Quantum theory suggests that it is the perceiver who determines the structure of existence. In other words, things are as they are because somebody—perhaps even us—expects that they will be this way. In his book *The Physics of Immortality,* Tipler proposes "that we identify the universal wave function constrained by the Omega Point Boundary Condition with the Holy Spirit." What is being said here is that there must be a large-scale perceiving force that governs the structure of the universe or it would not be here at all.

Tipler is not alone in his suggestion. Although the conservation of mass and energy is sufficient to explain motion without a first mover, it is not so easy to explain how mass would have resolved into discreet forms without a first perceiver. "It would appear that perhaps creation and observation are equally important at the beginning of time," theorizes Fred Alan Wolf in *Parallel Universes.* Indeed, it can even be rationally theorized that God's emerging awareness that the universe was possible created it, and God's interest may still be what motivates its evolution.

I think, at this point in the history of knowledge, it would be very foolish to reject out of hand the various theories that include a creator. And, given the apparent design behind the whole history of evolution, it would be equally foolish to suppose that the unfolding of the world does not remain a project of this consciousness.

There is going to be a time of great difficulty in human affairs, that is unavoidable. We have waited too long to address issues of population and the environment. We will feel the full expression of nature as the situation we are now in corrects itself.

On the far side of the time that is coming, I have glimpsed a new vision of mankind, one that is no longer trying to construct its life out of technology and inventions, but has surrendered to nature and taken its part in the mysterious consciousness that guides the unfolding of the world. I see this new mankind as compassionate, devoted to the service of Earth and spirit, and seeking toward the source of all real power, which is the increase of joy.

The School

Scientifically, we put all original causes far back in time.

We find ourselves in the world passing in time from moment to moment—a world of contradictions, of opposites, and, as it were, of half-truths. We know, in short, only a limited reality, which is characterized by passage in time. But the ultimate cause and origin of all things is not a million million years ago, it is outside time—Now.

—MAURICE NICOLL,
LIVING TIME

Time Traveler

IN THE WEEKS AFTER MY JOURNEY TO THE TELESCOPE, the doors of the secret school opened wide to me. I had survived the test and been initiated into experience at the place where the critical mysteries unfolded: the Olmos Basin. Here, in the strange silence of this place, along the bluffs and under the enormous old trees in the dead of the night, I was going to travel deep and far.

Many of the details came back after I located the secret school in November of 1995, but the broad outlines began to return during the previous summer. As I traveled around promoting *Breakthrough* and trying to keep up with the wave of UFO sightings that had started to unfold around the world during the weeks I was on my tour, I also found my childhood coming to life inside me again.

Although the UFO wave has continued and expanded massively, the tour ended in July, and Anne and I went to a rural resort.

Sitting under a tree and giving my mind up to repetitive prayer or meditating, I slowly regained the memories I am about to relate. Again and again, I recalled the night settling into its small hours, and waking up, and beginning the journey to the Basin. As I went back, this is what I found . . .

Night wind floods Texas, pouring up from the south so fresh and clean that it bears, over two hundred miles from the Gulf of Mexico, a clear scent of the sea. Outside my window the elm and mesquite and chinaberry trees sigh in their timeless tongues, and the cicadas and the frogs signal for mates.

I wake up to moonlight, rise up in the bed, and at once feel the sweet electricity of the night tingling through my body. I shudder from the pleasure of it. I am more than glad, I am in ecstasy. I'm going somewhere wonderful, and I know it well.

Sitting under that tree, I could taste the excitement that I felt then, the sheer delight of being that is the property of the young.

Candy raises her head curiously, warily, and snarls a bit. I touch her, take her small body in my arms, and stroke her, holding her like that until the sleep that I know will come envelops her. Then I get out of bed and go swiftly downstairs, avoiding the steps that creak, each of which I know well.

The house is so silent, so strange and new. I move past the telephone table in the hall, then through the dining room and the kitchen and out onto the kitchen porch, where I stop. I look up past the old mesquite that stands on the far side of the driveway, up into the starry sky. I inhale the deliciously secret air of the late night, then go into the storeroom where my bike is gleaming against the wall, my beloved Dunelt racer with the motto "Ride Awheel on Sheffield Steel" scripted in gold on its frame. I take the bike out into the driveway.

As I sat writing, I remembered it as if the event were still happening. It wasn't a generic event, but a specific night I was remembering: I wore light yellow pajamas that consisted of shorts and a T-top. The leather bike seat felt hard against my buttocks. The night was so quiet when the breeze died down that you could hear the fluttering wings of bats. I went down the driveway worrying that the clicking of the gears as the bike freewheeled would wake up the whole neighborhood. How perfect these memories appeared here in this quiet summer afternoon, with the breeze blowing as it did then, and the same rich emotions filling my heart. It was as if a record made and put away nearly half a century ago was being played for the first time.

I went through the silent streets, pedaling hard toward my destination. What I next recalled was so unexpected and incredible that I am not at all surprised at the degree of amnesia that has surrounded it all these years. Strangeness buried this memory, not trauma. It had nothing to do with any known technology, such as a virtual reality viewer. Rather, it was a step beyond such things, almost as if the earlier visions had been induced as a preparation for it—an artificial taste of something I was now tasting in reality.

As best I can, I will try to explain the state I was in. I have not been able to find it described elsewhere, although mystical philosopher Maurice Nicoll speculates about its existence in his book *Living Time and the Integration of the Life,* and such states seem integral to the idea-system of the Neoplatonist philosopher Plotinus.

As I rode my bouncing, rollicking bike across the Basin, I shed the child. It wasn't that I became older, but that my mind began to process what seemed to be impressions and experiences from more than one life at the same time. Soon I wasn't simply riding my bicycle, and I wasn't only in a wilderness area. At the same time I was doing these things, I was also running through the streets of a dark city that I knew belonged to the past.

The sense of the past faded, though, as I ran down the streets of this city. I came to understand that it was Rome. It had all the familiarity of a real and present place.

At the same time, the act of crossing the Basin on my bicycle also continued, but not in quite the same way. Neither life was "present." The child in San Antonio felt the other life as a vivid memory; a young man in the Rome of two thousand years ago taking a similar journey thought of the future child as a sort of spirit-of-self, a personal god who lived at once in his mind and his potential.

I can remember how comfortable this extremely strange state of being seemed. It was normal. I was used to it. As I rode in one life and walked in the other, I shifted the focus of my attention back and forth with complete ease. In the Basin, I was going to the benches. In Rome, I was going to a temple, one I knew was round and situated between two other temples. I knew that it was in a sacred precinct in a place called the Field of Mars, and that it was called the Temple of the Present Day. When I went to the Basin, I often went to this temple as well. In the level of consciousness that I was now remembering, I was not steeped as we usually are in linear time, but conscious in two presents in two parallel times instead.

To get to the temple, I went steadily downward, passing through narrow, unlit streets in a state of some considerable fear. Rome was dangerous. I went past a fig tree that stood in a small square, then along a dark colonnade I knew as the Colonnade of the Swan. After that, I crossed an open area that was packed with wagons and horses and shouting, cursing men. It smelled of hot manure and smoke, and was poorly lit by fires and a few guttering torches.

Then there was another colonnade, this one hung with oil lamps that gave a light so soft that it did little more than define the shadows.

I moved into an emptier area. As it did on the wilds of the Basin in San Antonio, a new moon shone down on this scene. There was a profound parallelism between the two moments that made me consider, sitting under the tree in the country contemplating the situation, that one of the reasons that the ancient stellar calendars man used in prehistory are so incredibly accurate is that they understood states like this, and used the calendars to find these exquisite temporal parallels.

As the boy was looking for a great, misshapen tree and a circle of benches, the man was looking for that round temple. In both places the moon was in exactly the same quarter, in exactly the same position in the sky.

In Rome, I soon saw the temple. It was small and extraordinarily graceful, and its shape and beauty impressed themselves powerfully upon my current memory. We do not build structures like this anymore.

The Texas night was sweet, but a sharp smoke hung in the Roman air, and there came from the streets behind me a great tumult of shouting and creaking, of horses and groaning labor. These were the night sounds of Rome, where, as the Roman part of me knew, haulage had just recently been banned in favor of pedestrian traffic during the daylight hours, and wagons could not use the streets except at night.

Both the body of the little boy in Texas and the young man in Rome were in the same state of vibrating, electric ecstasy. It was this state that held their minds above the flow of time.

The child who had started out from Elizabeth Road was no longer "me." He was just one of many people whom I was inhabiting across a great turn of centuries. Far from being a little boy, I was an old, old creature on a mission toward ecstasy, who sought—and seeks—across history for some permanent connection to joy.

The temple was a joyous sight, for I knew that I would meet within it a band of dear friends, people of whom I am part, and who have been part of me, since our beginning. As I walked, I shifted the child in Texas into memory and brought the young man in Rome to the surface.

I knew that, as the Texas child, I had arrived at our bench and was now sitting there with the Sister of Mercy, but the focus of my attention wasn't there anymore. Ahead, pale light glowed past the columns of the temple. I could see the warm stars of oil lamps hanging beneath its circular roof.

Intent that I arrive at the right moment, I went straight up the steps and entered through a wooden door so old it seemed like iron. The interior was lit by bigger oil lamps, which stood on graceful tripods around the edges of the room casting rich, lovely light.

In the center of the space was a tall statue of the Goddess of Fortune. Sitting around her were familiar friends, and standing before her was a young woman to whom I was deeply attached, although not as a lover. Rather, I saw her then much in the way I would see the Sister of Mercy in ages to come, as a person who had attained across her myriad lives the fabulous thing that I think we all unconsciously seek, which is to so completely embrace the larger meaning of reality that we become free of time.

She came forward with a pottery jar in her hands. It was about half filled with pale, fluffy fat. I dropped the filthy, slack linen tunic that I was wearing to the floor without a thought. The woman looked at me gravely for a moment, then began to slap the substance on my body. It was cold and slick, like sour, rank-smelling cold cream. As she covered me with it, there was a prickling sensation. Soon I began to feel loose in my body, as if my consciousness were about to fall out of my flesh.

She asked me if I could spend all night out. I told her that I had to be back before the first hour, and as I remembered this reply, the entire life I was living then also returned to my mind.

I was a Greek, about fifteen years old, the tutor of a wealthy child called Octavius, to whom I was deeply devoted. I was quite proud of his brilliance and felt a very strong sense of personal value that flowed from my association with him and his powerful, well-regarded family. I had absolutely no feeling of disquiet about being a slave. It was simply what I was and the idea of being something different held little interest for me.

I knew exactly what we were doing in the temple. The Roman state was falling into chaos because it had expanded too fast. We were seeking to create out of Octavius a man who would restore order on a long-term basis so that the Roman peace would serve as crucible for something very new, which we saw as a prophesied redemption for mankind. This could have been Christianity, but we did not think of it in a way that is recognizable to me now, and there were many redemptive religions in the Roman world.

Had Octavius not taken over the Roman Empire after the murder of his adopted father Julius Caesar (which happened near the Temple of the Present Day, oddly enough), it might well have collapsed before Jesus was even born rather than lasting five hundred years more, as it did. Under those chaotic conditions, his life would never have been enacted as it was, nor his teachings have gained the foothold that they did.

We were educating Octavius, and planned to use our knowledge of time to guide him through the dangerous period to come. Historically, Octavius became emperor at the age of eighteen, after a series of almost miraculously clever political maneuvers and adroit assassinations, especially considering that he was only seventeen and eighteen when he directed them.

A teenage boy created a new form of government, a novel mixture of republic and kingdom, and be-came master of the world's greatest empire. In history, there are no particular advisors identified who helped him. This pimply kid simply did it. But perhaps he had help that he kept secret, or did not fully understand.

Both in Rome and in San Antonio, I took my place among the others. In San Antonio, I sat on the bench beside my aged mentor. In Rome, I sat before her in her youth.

In Rome, she was a girl of unsurpassing beauty, perfect of limb, her dark hair rendered to grace and life by the soft light of the lamps. In San Antonio, she was of a shape more ancient than mortal man, swathed in black so that we children would not go mad with terror at the sight of her.

In both places, I began to accelerate. That is the only word for it. I remember a wave of nausea, then a sense of simply rushing up and right out of an opening in the roof of the temple.

The city that spread out around me was entirely familiar. I knew the streets, the monuments, the markets . . . and yet they were also spread with the wonder of the truly exotic. I was seeing them with two minds—one that belonged to a member of Roman society and another that had seen ancient Rome only as a ruin.

I was awake, then, truly awake—rising not only outside of my Roman and Texas times, but of all time . . . and, in the present, remembering the state with the greatest anguish. It is not only fear and strangeness that enforce our amnesia about such states. They are ecstatic, and to remember ecstasy that one no longer possesses is painful indeed.

We turn away. We are all turned away. But we can turn back . . . toward God, toward joy, into the arms of heaven. We can go home.

Even though in the Roman part of my consciousness I knew the city well, the presence of the Texas part made it also seem eerie and exotic and wonderful. Without doubt, it was one of the most beautiful human places ever created, as complex and richly constructed as modern Venice or Paris. It was not made of white marble, though, as the little Texas boy would have expected. The buildings were painted, which was amazing to the part of me observing from the bench in San Antonio. The part that was sitting under the tree in the present could look back through the memories of his boyhood self to the experience of his Roman identity and recognize one or two landmarks, chiefly the back of the temple of Jupiter Maximus, which seemed to have columns colored blue or purple and a gilt cornice. I also saw lit windows in what I think might have been a complex of villas above the Circus Maximus. I got a tantalizing glimpse of riches within: I could see painted walls, elegant, sparely designed chairs, and a tall tripod gleaming like gold on which stood an oil lamp.

Working with the memory at the country resort, I was also able to recall that I could not see the Flavian Amphitheater—the familiar Colosseum. It was not built until 80 A.D., which was probably over a hundred years after this experience, which I believe took place around 50 B.C.

Even as I rose above the city, I also knew that I was holding hands with my friends. We began to spin, moving faster and faster around the body of the goddess, orbiting with the majesty of moons circling a planet.

As we accelerated out of the temple and the sky above it, and beyond time, I began to see the world in a very different way. Time began to be added to everything as a new aspect of shape, with the result that things became long, reaching up out of the core of the Earth in enormously complex lines that emerged from a deep glow at the center of the planet. I saw it as the heart of the world.

In both Rome and Texas, we were praying. Because it resolves the issues of the moment, prayer is a key to escape from the illusions of life, and so a critical link to timeless reality. No matter the words, the faith, it is a connection with the vast source, the outflowing presence of deity. We prayed until it felt as if our Kyries were sounding in the ages. I took up the prayer under my tree, gazing across the quiet lake as my mind came unchained.

Then the lesson began to end. It ended in Rome, it ended in San Antonio, and it ended at the country resort. In all three places, I began to return.

It is gray dawn and I am very tired and my skin is oily and foul. I drop my tunic down over my body and cinch it with the cloth braid. I lace up my sandals, which are also shabby. I'm uneasy; I have overstayed the permission of my master and I know it. We all know it, we little band. There are thirteen of us, including the maiden upon whom our rituals are centered. She is now chewing nuts of some sort. She's tired and her eyelids are swollen. The group of us talk together, planning our next meeting. We speak a rough form of Latin—very simple vocabulary, very limited in verbal expression and grammatical subtlety. Because my daily work involves language, I would greatly enjoy expressing myself better, but not all of the companions could follow the Latin, and we have many different native languages.

It's cool, but none of us have cloaks. We are backstairs people. Officially, the temple precinct is closed to us, and we could be executed for blasphemy if we were discovered here. I go off across the marble piazza that surrounds the three temples, of which ours is one.

Now I am moving quickly along the Via Recta, heading into the center of the city. I will pass down the Via Lata, then through the forae and onto the Arguiletum, thence into the fine residential quarter that is on the Collis Viminalis.

It takes half an hour to make this journey. At one point, I pass the small chamber where my charge goes to school and see that the class is already in session. He might be beaten by the sour old man who drills them in philosophy and oratory. If he is, I will be in my turn, by his father's direction.

I run, clambering up a steep road that is so rutted and wet that filth covers my feet. There were chairs that could be hired which would have gotten me home faster, and the men who carried them stood about in doorways, but I had no money, and perhaps it was not wise for a man of my station to allow himself to be carried without explicit orders from home. I can recall struggling along in the wet, going past large buildings with stone boxes of flowers in the windows. I passed a place where they were making sausages that smelled of liver and were shaped like little bags. I recall men struggling with a collapsed wall, pulling at piles of bricks while a Roman in his toga stood by, as silent and dangerous, I thought, as a coiled serpent.

I felt very much a member of the family to whom I belonged, but also an outsider in this Roman place. I was property of the Romans, and envied them the iron ring, which I believe was the mark of citizenship. Although it appears from my own memory that Romans must have worn such rings, I have not turned up anything in the literature about Roman life that supports this.

I went into a wider area, the Forum Romanorum, later to become the Forum of Augustus. There was a colonnade around it, with two tiers of arches, and inside were many different sorts of merchants, among them people selling rather surprising things such as ice that was kept in stone containers that drained water out into the street. There were fountains running with fairly weak streams of water. More Romans were here in their togas, standing in small groups. These were unsmiling men, dark men, and I can well recall how I feared them. I felt exposed, as if each of them knew me and what I had done, and would report me. I lived in a large household, though, a huge household, and could reasonably hope that I had not yet been listed.

I came to a certain corner, and there hanging on

hooks on a wall were whips. These were used by men who went from house to house like milkmen to punish slaves.

I entered our house. Within, there was hazy smoke, a heavy odor of cooking—spice, hot milk, a roasting smell. The walls were painted with scenes of country life. It was a very elegant house. I stayed to side corridors, moving with my head down when I passed any room where there might be members of the family. I dreaded my name being taken down, because I had seen the whip in use and did not think that I could survive it. I knew, also, that many of its victims wasted away later, even if they did live through the ordeal.

Finally, I parted the thick curtain that closed the door of my charge's bedroom, went in, and found him sitting in his bedclothes, not even having left the blocky wooden couch where he slept. He stared at me with wide, amazed eyes, as if I had surprised him very much by my absence. I went about my work, calling his body servants to prepare him, lifting him onto a little wooden step where they would change his clothes and dress his hair while I drilled him in his temporal verbs. I can remember saying, "The idea of time in the language of the Hellenes . . ."

Then I was back in the secret school in Texas. We were getting up from our benches, hugging each other, telling our teacher good-bye. She sat slumped, her head down, as motionless as if she were dead. We were used to it, hugging her unresponsive body anyway. The cloth of her habit was rough-woven, not soft like the habits of regular nuns.

After that night, Rome became even more obsessively fascinating to me than Egypt. It was from then on as if my attention was divided between the two lives, one being lived out in late republican Rome, the other in San Antonio.

Perhaps the reason that these two lives joined may be that they take place in times of historical parallel. Just as the Roman republic was in danger of falling into chaos, so the American republic is in such danger now. But there is a deeper reason, for these two lives were not the only ones that merged together in the timelessness of the secret school. There was a third life, lived a very long time ago, that also parallels the ones lived in Rome and now. It also takes place at the change of two ages. Contained in it is the deepest secret of all, the explanation of why our very reality seems to be collapsing just now, drowned beneath waves of UFOs, near-death experiences, and stunningly powerful encounters with the unknown.

It also explains why so many of us see danger ahead.

COMMENTARY ON THE SEVENTH LESSON

Mind Outside of Time

For most of my life, I have unconsciously tried to recapture my Roman memories. I went to Rome in 1968, drawn to search for a round temple that contained a beautiful statue of a woman. After wandering around in the ruins for a few days, I finally settled on the so-called Temple of Vesta, an intact structure near the Temple of Portunus that was actually dedicated to Hercules. I can recall going into its portico and walking around and around it, trying to understand why it drew me so strongly. It wasn't the right temple, though. I knew that even then.

In 1968 I recalled only that the temple I sought was round. At the country resort, as I thought back, I saw it much more clearly. It was set between two other temples. I recalled that it had been called the Temple of Time, or perhaps the Temple of the Present. This was enough to enable me to set out looking through old books to see if I could find it.

At first, no luck. Then I found a book called *Rome 2000 Years Ago,* published in Italy in the mid-eighties. It describes a group of temples in the Campus Martius, the Field of Mars, one of which is called the *Aedes Fortunae Huiusce Diei*—the Temple of the Present Day.

Not only was the name of the temple very close, so was its shape, and its placement in the Campus Martius certainly fit the mysterious relationship between my whole experience and Mars.

In the temple was an enormous statue of the Goddess Fortuna, who had a very interesting place in the Roman Pantheon. She was mistress of present time, the goddess of the moment. Since time travel appears to be a matter of expanding the present to include more and more of the past and the future, the name was appropriate to a place where ritual movements through time might have been undertaken.

That I would find a specific temple that meets so exactly the specifications of name, shape, and location that I remembered from life in the secret school is as oddly suggestive of an unexpected level of factual reality as the rest of these stories.

I know that it all sounds impossible, like the work of an overactive imagination. I know that my evidence is fragile. But I am not asking that my stories be taken as fact. I am asking, as an honest man, that the effort I am making to relate what appear to me to be real memories not simply be rejected out of hand.

Later, I will include visions of the immediate future sufficiently detailed to either validate or disqualify my claims in just a few years, so time will evaluate my efforts for me.

What this lesson involved was a completely new way of being aware of something that I suspect is commonplace to all of us, but intentionally ignored. We stay away from it because it is dangerous to the sense of spontaneity that living inside time offers, which we use to create change in ourselves.

The story of our manipulation of Octavius may be an example of how mankind actually goes about creating history. Judging from it, we do not try to make everything beautiful and sweet and good. It has to be hard, it has to give us ample opportunity to expose our souls to genuine goodness and real wrongdoing. If so, then this world is a school indeed, and we ourselves are both teachers and students.

We have too many problems now, however, to enjoy the luxury of time blindness. We've got to see the consequences of what we do in the world much more clearly and objectively if we are going to survive even into the next generation. We have to extend our reach in time both backward and forward, to see our real history so that we can truly understand ourselves, and learn to prophesy so that we can prepare the way for our future to manage itself well.

This is not only about short-term survival. I want to see mankind injected deeply into the future. I want to see humanity gain a permanent place in this world, to persist not for a few centuries or millennia, but for the ages.

What I experienced on that night was the fact that it is possible to enter one's past lives in a completely unexpected way. These lives are not necessarily dead. They are only dead if you look back at them down the tunnel of time. But if you leave the time stream altogether, then they turn out to be very much alive. When you ascend above time, it isn't that everything seems like the past, but that the present expands to contain all events.

Thus, when I walked the streets of Rome, they were very real streets, as real as the path in the Olmos Basin, as present as the tree in the country had been last summer, or this moment is right now.

In this sense, there is no time. We create the present. It's an invention. But we can reinvent it, and if we do that on a large enough scale, we may gain living contact with our past and future, and even become able to change them.

My mysterious visitors once displayed an image to me that communicated their concept of time. They do not see the future ahead and the past behind. To them, the future is like a pool of water to their right, the past a block of ice to their left. The present is the force that fixes the potential that lies in the future, turning it into the ice of the past. They seek back into the past to melt, change, and re-create, then refreeze their history. Using this process, they can to an extent repair problems and imbalances in their present time.

They can prophesy, but this does not involve predicting things that are absolutely inevitable. Rather, a prophecy is a warning. Its purpose is to identify dangerous future situations that are inevitable given present conditions, so that those conditions can be changed. In this sense, the best of all prophets must always be wrong, because the dangers that they see are averted by their prophecies.

We have forgotten this, and so lost not only our belief in prophecy, but our ability to identify the real thing.

After I remembered the lesson of simultaneous lives, I began to wonder if the present could actually contact the past. My past self was somewhat aware of the future one, and the future one could see the one in the past. But could they actually change anything?

During my ninth summer, I began reading Roman history voraciously. Given an experience like that, who wouldn't become fascinated? But there may have been more to it than that. If I am right about what was going on at night in the Temple of the Present Day, the past knew—or knows—a great deal more about time than we do.

If the temple is a sort of target, I doubt that it would be the only one in history. It may be that many exist.

Robert Bauval, coauthor of *The Orion Mystery,* a book that points out a relationship between the placement of the pyramids on the Giza plateau to the constellation Orion, has said in an interview, "It seems that we have a device that was built to work with time." Author Gordon-Michael Scallion reports that he had a vision of the construction of the Great Pyramid while at Giza, as vivid as the journeys back in time that I and so many others experience.

To move around in time, it seems useful to remember these places in great detail, and to do it in the context of a powerful physical and emotional state. As a child, I would enter this state when I approached the secret school, and now that I have remembered what it was like, I have tried to re-create it.

The foundation of the state is very clear to me. It's joy. When the visitors said to me, "Have joy," they uttered the most powerful of all words, because all real freedom—in fact, the freedom that we need to break out of the bondage of time and space—begins with joy.

The reason that the secret school unfolds in the lives of children, it seems to me, is that they have easy access to this emotion. But how can we adults gain access to real joy in this dark world of ours? It cannot be accomplished by denying or ignoring reality. The cruel lie that all is somehow well because we "choose" the misfortunes that enter our lives—a notion popular in certain New Age and religious circles—is nothing but another form of denial.

What is joy? It isn't happiness, which is something that we take. Joy seems to be a much deeper state, something we surrender to. We can find it in the eyes of our children, in the beauty of the world around us, in the depths of our own souls. Tasting it is a matter of returning. What has not been known before is that a state of joy is actually a state of power. One cannot find joy without becoming objective about oneself and life, and accepting the idea that, while good is to be desired and evil resisted, it is also true that both have a place.

When I was first seeking this more ecstatic state, I had what is perhaps the most beautiful experience of my life, one that suggested to me that there are amazing powers available to us when we truly give ourselves up to joy.

After I remembered that night in the Temple of the Present Day, I began trying to return to Rome again while at the country resort. There was a brief, vivid journey back, in which I was walking with Octavius to the school. It was very early in the morning, and as we entered the small room that opened onto a side street, I saw the teacher verbally chastising another boy and heard the other students deriding the old man with irony in their voices—because they were the sons of citizens and he was, of course, a slave.

Then something happened that greatly intensified my joy, and so gave me the power to maneuver more freely in space-time. I was lying in a chair, once again experimenting with states of energized relaxation, when I suddenly felt myself change. I began to vibrate, and by visualizing colors on higher and higher frequencies—letting my mind move from dark blue through violet—I caused the rate of vibration to increase.

I released my thoughts, turning my attention to my body, concentrating on my solar plexus, for the moment abandoning the cares of life. What came was not what I had hoped, which was a conscious return to the Temple of the Present Day. Rather, I found myself reliving another moment, a very special one. This is a moment of a sort so hidden by mystery and amnesia that we have hardly even speculated about it.

I found myself in a sky of the purest sunlit blue. Below me, fine little clouds, bright white in the light, flowed up from the south. Farther below, a green canopy of trees was tossed by summer wind. Under that canopy, I could glimpse the roofs of houses.

Falling like a lazy bit of pollen, I drifted downward. I was being drawn as if by a gentle, thrilling magnetism. Slowly I dropped down until I could hear the sigh of the breeze in the trees, farther into the smiling light until I passed through the green shelter into the shady intimacy of a summer afternoon.

Close by, a cicada trilled, its voice rising with what I heard as passion. In that moment, passing among the leaves of the trees, past the bark of mesquite limbs, I saw my old house that I had known as a boy. It was white-painted brick, standing silently in the afternoon thrall.

Such a delicious feeling of secrecy came over me then, as if I must at all costs conceal myself from every living thing. But it was a happy secrecy, like the feeling one gets as a child playing hide-and-seek in the shadows of evening. I was at peace in a way that I had never before tasted, but which has never left me, not since remembering. In the deep of love that I felt, there was also a sense of lightness that told me a truth about myself and all of us: even though we are an ancient race, we are also young.

Then I saw a window with a half-drawn shade. I began moving toward it. Before I went in, I looked back toward a golden billow of clouds that seemed somehow to conceal our true home. I went in the window, passing right through the screen, the glass, and the shade, and into the dim yellow room beyond. Below me there was a bed, and on it a woman sleeping in her negligee.

I looked down upon the small, sleeping woman with the little dog beside her, feeling happiness that I had found her and joy that she was to be my mother. The difference between the two states was completely clear. I had gained the happiness for myself. The joy was being given to me in the form of a mother to bring me into life.

The dog looked up, gazing at me with her dark, rich eyes, and I saw concern there, a slight confusion—and then I was in a pale red room and something was booming off in the distance.

This memory has become one of my deepest and most profound personal treasures. The whooshing, thudding, sloshing reality of the womb, the rise and fall of voices outside, the soft call of music from the bedside radio, and all the time this dialogue between us, a conversation that began at the first moment of our meeting and has never yet stopped, not even with her death.

The joy of tasting this level of relationship was like a kind of fuel. Feeling the power of it, in this deeply surrendered state, I understood for the first time the true tragedy and danger of evil, but also how to get free of it by transforming it into a tool for growth.

What denies us access to joy is evil. Evil works by binding us to its dark weight. It is this that imprisons us in the three-dimensional world, trapped in its narrow, linear illusion of reality. It is also true, though, that working against the weight can make us strong.

Whenever I taste the joy of the womb, I can fly free of all that binds me. Remembering all of these things about the past, I began to wonder if we could communicate with it, even change it. There are fascinating paradoxes involved here. For example, if we go back and change the past, how can we know that we've done it, as we must already be living with the outcome of the changes?

I had an experience that I think might have been intended to teach me something about the degree to which we can actually enter and affect the past. The event happened in August of 1995, and may have actually been *part of* the effort that the temple group was making to bring Octavius to power so many thousands of years ago.

It involved communication with a man who was going to die in a matter of minutes, and—significantly—never could have had the opportunity to tell anybody what had happened. However, the few moments that I delayed him could well have been critical.

Cicero, the man with whom I had contact, was an orator and powerful member of the Roman senate. He was a leading champion of the republic and one of the principal opponents of Octavius. As the last defender of the Roman republic, he remains one of Western history's most important figures. In the end, his ideas did not prevail, and he was assassinated by his young rival.

The death of Cicero and the destruction of the

republic were critically important to Roman history, and so also to our own. I knew, even before my journey backward happened, that something important was about to take place. As I was sitting at my desk in the middle of the afternoon, I began to feel a powerful, pulsating vibration go through my body.

I went to a couch in our cottage at the resort and lay back. Now the vibration in my body rose to a tingling, which began sweeping through me like waves. It felt as if I was becoming, somehow, a thing of electricity. It seemed that I might actually lose my physical shape if I didn't keep concentrating on it, as if I suddenly had to maintain a form that I normally could not change.

Then I realized that I was seeing somebody, a man in a toga. The vision appeared real enough to allow me to feel that I was back in Rome, but not in my Roman self. I was something else, an electric creature, a thing that seemed composed of pure ecstasy.

At first I did not recognize who I was seeing. He appeared as a washed-out image beside a wall with high windows in it. As he became clearer, though, I saw that he was dreadfully afraid, his complex face drained of hope. I was aware that I was standing in front of this man, and that I was wearing a tunic. I seemed smaller than him.

I felt as if I was coming to this man with a message that was a sort of gift, and that I could give it to him because his life was at its end and he would be compelled by his fate to keep my secret. It appeared that this degree of communication with the past would have been impossible if much more latitude than that had been allowed. It seemed terribly, terribly important that he never tell anybody about this, and the sense of intimate secrecy that was involved was not unlike the sense of thrilling stealth that accompanied my descent into the womb.

I said, "I'm here to tell you that you and your works are still remembered two thousand years in the future."

He stared at me. His face went blank. A moment later there were cries echoing from somewhere and he went hurrying off. Then I saw him being ridden down at the edge of a woods by four soldiers. I remember those horsemen with their tunics and their distinctive arched Roman saddles and how fast they seemed to ride as they raced to prevent him from being carried into the dense woods by his slaves.

Historically, Cicero was beheaded by soldiers of Octavius at the edge of a wood near his country villa. Had the old man lived, Octavius could never have achieved the degree of control that he did. Cicero's escape on that day might well have meant that he could have rallied forces to his own defense.

I wonder if the moment that I delayed him was needed by the horsemen. If so, then the future changed itself in a massive way by simply injecting itself into a few seconds of the past.

Contemplating such an enormous thought, I am left to wonder how the world actually works. Stephen Hawking used to ask where time's tourists were. Perhaps they are everywhere and in all times, stretching a moment here, shortening one there, as this wonderful mystery called humanity journeys across the ages creating itself.

The Human Past

REMEMBERING THE JOURNEY OUTSIDE OF TIME WAS
another step. Afterward, I began to recall more. I
recalled that the school had a very definite structure,
that there had been nine lessons each summer that I
attended.

So I had two more yet to recall from age nine. But
for some reason I didn't want to remember them.
Above all, I did *not*. The result of this was a total
blank, and a return of the feeling that had worried
me from the beginning, that this was nothing more
than an act of the imagination, an interesting but
essentially worthless exercise.

I struggled with myself, trying meditation, bar-
gaining with myself, writing random thoughts.
Finally, I went alone to the ruins of the secret school,
to try to extract the memories by retracing my movements. It was a sunny afternoon, and I climbed the
arrow-straight cut to the old tree, then sat beneath it.
Its leaves rustled, and I tried to imagine what it must

know, all the things it must have seen in its vast lifetime. I wished that it would tell me about a certain night nearly half a century ago when a little boy had seen a whole hidden past.

I could almost hear the faint click and clatter of the bicycles as we struggled up the path with them, see the shadowy line of children coming up the steps of time.

Suddenly I could just *taste* that sense of secrecy. In those days I had *known about* the school. Of course I had, I had thought about it all the time! It hadn't been concealed from me then. I knew perfectly well what I did with my summers, and so did the other kids who were involved.

We were a secret club, a little band of adventurers. We never spoke about it, not even with each other . . . except in the whispers of the night, when sometimes we camped out and went to the Basin together.

Sitting there, thinking about those days, I brought some of my companions to mind. A few of them are still close friends. Two live in South Texas in fairly close contact with the visitors, others seem to have forgotten everything, others have disappeared from my life.

Remembering their faces, I began also to remember some of the structure of the school. There were graduations and admissions. Kids came in for the first time, kids finished.

Subsequently, I made a list of all the people I remember from my own classes. Two besides myself are aware that we "did something in the Basin." So far, none of them, and none of the people Ed Conroy found who went to the Basin, have remembered much detail. Besides those that met in the Basin, there must have been—and still be—many such circles, and one of my hopes is that this book will touch memory in others so deep and clear that the level on which it is a true story about real, factual events will become more apparent. I wish that I could say that some of the people whom I remember attending classes with me shared more detailed recollections, but it just isn't true.

I sat listening to the sighing leaves of the old live oak and trying to evoke memory without also bringing my imagination to bear. Memories such as these are like objects moving too fast to be seen. The fact that they cannot be perceived directly doesn't mean that they aren't real. But the imagination is such a snare . . .

The tree sighed, traffic on a nearby expressway hissed its way toward oblivion, insects rustled in the leaves around me. Had I really done this?

Oh, yes. Yes, I had certainly come here in the midnights of my childhood. That happened; I would defend that fact.

I looked on up the path, toward the ruined benches. Who was our teacher? I went on up to the ruined benches, sat down where I remembered my corner. I noticed that they weren't actually benches, but a structure of some sort. There was a garbage tailing nearby, where trash from the retired sisters' home had been thrown in the old days.

I closed my eyes, thinking of the Sister of Mercy. Immediately, I remembered that she was incredibly old. I touched the board beside me, and I remembered . . .

Our meetings began with a prayer, and I can hear her rattling whisper: *"Sicut erat in principio, et nunc, et semper: et in saecula saeculorum."* As it was in the beginning, is now, and ever shall be: world without end.

Now I see her quite clearly. She was thin and slight and had hard bones. She didn't smell like starch like the other nuns. She smelled like loam. We used to give sisters fancy soap as a Christmas gift, but you would never have given the Sister of Mercy anything like that, she was much too plain and simple.

There was something about her body—a tickling vibration—that we really liked. We all wanted to be near her, and sitting beside her was a big reward. When she touched us, it would transform us into a state where we felt spectacularly, deliciously alive, as if every cell was conscious.

One by one, she would touch us, grabbing our hips, our faces. I remember that I saw inside her wimple once, and it looked as if a giant moth was staring out at me. My whole being rocked with terror.

We would get up and go round and round, dancing. The sister danced with us, her habit whooshing in the dark. We danced the backward dance, going past the ages, deep into time. And as we danced in 1954, we joined to our dance in Rome, and to another dance, longer past.

Everything is dance, she would say—dance of time; dance of life; dance of fate; dance of air, water, and light; dance of fire and future; history dance. Evil, love, good, hate, holy, cruel—all the dances are *the dance*.

Graduates were called dancers. I am a dancer now.

Remembering that, I finally feel that I am getting to something specific—down to the darkest place, the thing that doesn't want to come out.

I listen to the trees, I look off down the path. I wish that she were here again, with her thin old shoulder to lean on that was really so very strong.

Suddenly, I remembered that we had tests, and that helps. It helps a great deal, because I realize that what I am having so much trouble focusing on was one of the tests.

One August night we were supposed to go to the very deep past. The lives we were to enter unfolded twelve thousand years ago, when the zodiac crossed to Leo.

We had been studying the zodiac, which she said was a scientific instrument called a long-measure. There were other long-measures once, including some that measured every second all the way back to the beginning of time. We didn't have to go that far, though. All we had to do was cross a barrier of ignorance . . .

To go somewhere in time, you generally need to know that place, to be able to visualize it, to touch it with your senses until it becomes your present. Smells, tastes, bits of music—all of these things help. The test was to go to a place lost beyond memory.

How to do this? Close your eyes, do the inner looking, turn on your time searchlight, seek back. I could shine mine on Romans, on Egyptians, even on dinosaurs. But how could I shine it on something I didn't already know about?

She could put pictures in your head, and suddenly

I remember an incredibly vivid picture of being pushed off the wall of the Bastille. I am tied up, I am struggling, the terror is horrible—and then I'm falling, there is screaming wind—I hit, I bounce—a flash of agony—

But this night was not about the French Revolution, it was about falling, helpless and blind, into the unknown. I went into an era of man that was another manifestation of consciousness entirely—a world that was so completely different from this one that it is practically impossible to understand.

What I got first were snapshots: a group of people standing beside a quiet inland lake, the sun rushing across the sky.

Rushing. But that can't be, so I push it away.

What I expect to see are cavemen and mammoths and—wonder of them all—a saber-toothed tiger. But I do not see these things. Instead, something very different appears—a whole, complete world that is in no way our modern world. I see it only for a moment, then it is gone. But the color, the complexity, the sense of life—it's all quite amazing.

I see cities, but they seem isolated and enclosed, much more so than at any time in our recorded history. Most of the people are outside the cities and live primitive lives. Those inside, though, exist in a state that even today would seem like magic.

This is not a good world. The oppressions of Rome are kind compared to what chains these people. Their knowledge may be greater than what we have now, but they have used their intelligence to enslave their own souls. This world is engaged in some sort of obsessive project, and I know what it is. They are trying to escape. They are trying to break the chains that bind them to the Earth.

I go closer, I enter myself as I was then—and I find that it is a very troubled self. I am afraid. We are all dreadfully afraid. We have deep mines, and in them are detectors that tell us what is happening in the center of the Earth. I know that Earth's core is crystalline iron, not molten as we think in 1995. We understand how even the slightest blow to the planet's surface, correctly delivered, can cause this crystal to begin vibrating, and when it vibrates it creates movements in the mantle like waves in a storm. When struck, Earth behaves like a plastic.

We use these detectors to tell us things about the Earth that our present age no longer understands. From them, we can determine exactly what is going to happen to the planet in the future, and we know that there is going to be an impact, and we know exactly when it will come, to the day.

Now I understand why the Sister sent me to the colliding galaxies at the beginning of the summer, so that I would not be too overwhelmed by the sense of doom that fills this place. I am at the shore of a clear, still lake that we call Time Eternal. It is shallow, this lake, no more than three or four feet deep, and it is artificial. By watching the behavior of the water, we can measure tiny variances in the rotation of the planet. Our astronomical observations are so exact that we can determine the precise orbit and speed of planets, of any object that we can see.

We do not look at the cosmos as benign or space as empty. Our view is very much more fearful. We are aware of many dangers in space. We perceive the slow precession of the equinox as a mill that usually works very smoothly, but sometimes goes berserk. We fear that this is about to happen again, and we are watching the skies.

If it does, we know that mankind will suffer extra-ordinary destruction, as has happened before. Human civilization is cursed to rise to a certain point, only to be destroyed by these periods of insta-bility. All of our knowledge will be lost, and to the future it will look as if we have never been.

Part of what we are doing is to try to build stoneworks that will survive the cataclysm and take with them a coded message to the future, so that the people who are next threatened will read and under-stand the danger they are in. We have also created a sort of mechanism that exists in our genes, that will come to light when the equinox is opposite its cur-rent position and the world is again threatened. This device is the secret school, and the time for which it was created is when Pisces moves into Aquarius.

Even the vast difference between the nature of the two signs—the one the most structured in our calen-dar and the next the least so—suggests that they have been placed in juxtaposition to communicate a change that will be extremely profound.

We don't know what our warning will mean to those future people. We do know that they will mostly be lost in ignorance, wandering helplessly, as a conse-quence of what is about to happen to us. Never-theless, we intend to reach out across time to them, to warn them and call them back to the knowledge that is buried within them.

We are afraid because of something that we see

happening in our own skies. As the Earth moves toward the next house of the zodiac, a comet also approaches. We understand the relationship between its coming and the process of precession; we know that this object has been here before, and we fear the consequences.

It is close now, a huge white smear in the sky. It lights the night like a hundred moons. It is so enormous, we know that the earth will not survive a direct impact. We pray against even small parts of it breaking off and coming toward us. We send our will against it, we send prayers.

Day by day, it gets closer. Building efforts have been under way for some time, based on our understanding of what the end of the age might mean. We recognize that we will be destroyed.

Despite the fear, the sorrow, I am feeling a sense of relief. What is impossible for us is to grow and evolve. We know too many secrets, in a way, to allow us any freedom of action. Our world has a defeated purpose: it knows so much that nothing can surprise us and there can thus be no change or growth. In a sense, we have no further questions, and this is why our civilization is used up.

We count the days. Finally, we know the hour, the minute, the second of impact. I am with friends and family. We are standing and waiting by the Lake of Time Eternal.

When the end comes, it is incredibly fast. It appears like an enormous lightning bolt—a shaft of white fire tinged with violet that fills half the sky with its radiance. It is so intense that I can feel its heat against my face.

Then, in the opposite quadrant of the sky, the sun suddenly rises. It is majestic but very fast—far too fast—and its appearance causes people to cry out in horror. In fact, it moves up and across the horizon in a matter of a few minutes. It is sickening to see, sailing through an eerily silent sky. When it drops below the opposite horizon, the stars come out.

It grows rapidly very dark—but then, moments later, dawn begins again. Then the moon races across the sky, followed by a series of false dawns that seem to move from south to north, if the directions I am remembering have any meaning.

About fifteen minutes after the impact, the lake disappears, the water hissing away into the gloom. The horizon has begun to glow steadily, and clouds are beginning to boil upward, clouds that remind me, as I remember them, of the summer storm I saw in June of 1954. It is no wonder that I saw a world in that storm; riding it, I suppose, were the ghosts of my own distant past.

At that point, the little boy in the secret school in 1954 was in agony, because I understood that this was not only about something that happened ages ago, but also something that was going to happen again, something terrible that happened regularly, that was part of the life of the world, that could destroy everything in an instant.

I had seen the sun and moon bouncing around in the sky and storms coming, and I wanted to go home and hide under my bed with Candy and never come out. But the Sister would not let me hide, and I went back even deeper.

This time I saw the crisis from above.

I saw cities thrown down to ruin because the strike set up vibrations that swept out across the planet, which turned on its axis, once, twice, three times. Then hell itself seemed to crack open. The whole earth exploded into a maelstrom of dust. Plains turned into mountains, water flooded valleys, seabeds rose shining into the air.

As I watched from above, I also saw myself in the disaster, looking out into the thickening dark, looking toward an immense black cliff of water coming toward me. It must have been a thousand feet high. It was simply incredible to see, an unimaginable monolith surging through the murk.

I recall a rising cataract of sound, a rolling mist that became driving, pouring rain that became a thunder of water. And then I ascended also, rising into death. The little boy on the bench shrieked. The man I am now sighs, remembering.

The destruction of the Permian, which involved no conscious creatures, had a curiously precise, indifferent quality to it, like an act of surgery. As the richly conscious world of ten thousand B.C. died, there was a very different feeling, a sense of enormous regret.

We possessed a great store of knowledge and a way of thinking about nature that is fundamentally more true than what we have at present. After that world was killed, we set off across the long chaotic adventure that we call history, our purpose being to find wisdom enough to create a world that would last.

I cannot recall exactly how that particular night ended at the school, but it must have been like the others—a ride home along the edge of dawn, then a short sleep, and staying in bed late listening to the birds and watching golden motes of dust float through the pure morning light. Mornings after I went to the secret school, I would stay by myself, trying to cope with feelings and the memories.

Had I known what awaited me during the final weeks of that summer—visions of a future that is now becoming true before my eyes—I do not know if I could have borne it.

COMMENTARY ON THE EIGHTH LESSON

A Lost World

This encounter with an unconventional vision of the human past in part reflects the familiar legend of Atlantis, a legend that, for most of my life, I have dismissed as folklore.

But is it? The much-debated story has evolved in recent years into a group of theories about the past that suggest that, even if man was not fully civilized prior to the rise of Egypt, there were powerful builders present on this planet then—so powerful, in fact, that some of their feats still cannot be duplicated.

Not only that, there are ample suggestions both in mythology and paleoanthropology that the human past is not by any means fully understood. For example, the Vedic literature of India contains the concept that there have been many prior ages of man, receding much further into the past than is presently believed.

A rather interesting case can be made for this idea. At a number of places in Europe, among them

Thenay and Aurillac in France, Boncelles in Belgium, and Suffolk in England, eoliths, or worked stones, have been found that apparently date from the Miocene era, over 5 million years ago. The workmanship on these stones has been dismissed as the result of natural forces, because admitting their possible human origin would entirely ruin the theory of human evolution that has been generally accepted by twentieth-century paleontology. In recent years, as various branches of science gradually fell into the trap of ignoring and suppressing evidence that did not fit prevailing theories, the fact that competent scientists once accepted that these artifacts were genuine has been conveniently forgotten.

In 1935 the eminent paleontologist J. Reid Moore said in reference to the findings in Suffolk, "It becomes necessary to recognize a much higher antiquity for the human race."

Could this mean that the entire process of evolution into technological culture has taken place before, and that the remains of our previous achievements have been so completely destroyed that we cannot even recognize or find them now?

If so, then perhaps the ancient myth of Hamlet's Mill has some truth in it. The Hamlet of legend was a benevolent figure who, at unpredictable intervals, flew into berserk rages and destroyed everything around him. The mythical mill has been brilliantly identified by Giorgio De Santillana and Hertha Von Dechend in their book *Hamlet's Mill* as the precession of the equinox. This is the slow backward rotation of the poles around a hypothetical axis perpendicular to the sun. It is the precession of the equinox that, over the 26,000 years of the zodiacal calendar, moves the pole slowly backward through the calendar's houses.

Precession occurs because the true axis of the earth is tilted. The tilt is what causes our seasons, as the Earth faces first the northern and then the southern hemisphere toward the sun. While the axial tilt causes four seasons in a year, it drives the pole backward around the zodiac much more slowly. For the north pole to pass from one house to the previous takes 2,160 years.

In ancient times, it was believed that the period when the pole was transiting between houses was a dangerous one. This is not inherently so, as there is nothing different about the axial shift just because the pole is moving from one house of the zodiac to the next. And indeed, as the planet passes from one house to the next, nothing untoward happens—usually.

Something did happen around ten thousand B.C., however, that is probably commemorated by all the flood and catastrophe legends that emerge out of our prehistory. In my vision of the deep past, two things were taking place: the planet was moving from one house to the next, *and* a large cometary object of some kind was approaching. This object came close enough that there was obviously a major disturbance in the planet's rotation and there may have been fragments that impacted earth as well. The result was the total destruction of the civilization that existed then. Its great achievements were left only as legends and myths.

Could it be that the deep past created the zodiac to

warn its own distant future of the danger that would arise when a certain object passed close to the Earth? Were the houses of the zodiac devised around the constellations that they commemorate to mark the times when this object reappears, and warn of its passing? Certainly the houses of the zodiac were not named because the constellations actually look like the figures they are supposed to represent. Pisces, for example, is just a vague little clump of stars, completely impossible to distinguish as fish.

It is worth noting here that many of the constellations are the same all over the world, with many similar names in the Americas, China, the ancient Middle East, and Europe. The Great Bear, Pegasus, and Taurus, among others, are all shared. It is difficult to put this down to coincidence, and it may mean that the zodiac, or some important parts of it, predate all of these civilizations. "The truth is that the cultural origins of the constellations is largely unknown," comments Linda Therkorn, an archaeologist at the University of Amsterdam. The first clear instances of a sky calendar divided into twelve houses occur in ancient Sumeria.

I wonder if the zodiac was not created by an ancient science as a calendar and warning device that acquired its mythology only as its real function was forgotten. This sort of decline into ignorance can be illustrated with the Sphinx. Its meaning was lost to memory by the time of the ancient Greeks, whereupon it entered their mythology as a beast that waylaid travelers on the road to the Greek city of Thebes and killed them if they couldn't answer its riddle. As always, the decline was into fear and superstition.

The zodiac is highly sophisticated. For example, its creators had to be able to measure the movement of stars over generations in order to achieve the exact measurements that they did. Their motive certainly wasn't agricultural: the calendar measures millennia, not seasons.

Why? What purpose has a 26,000-year calendar that is divided into segments over 2,000 years long? If it is not to measure the seasons of the year, then perhaps there are greater seasons, seasons of the Earth or of the soul or of man, seasons so large that the scale to which we have declined as a civilization has made us lose sight of them. Maybe that is why this immensely careful creation has become encrusted in superstition and scientific ignorance. Its very real calendrical capabilities are seen—and dismissed—as magic.

Presently, we are moving from Pisces to Aquarius, which science tells us has no special significance, but it would be reassuring if we could find some way to determine why the zodiac was created. Since late 1995, there has been an unusual amount of cometary activity in our solar system. Jupiter has received a dramatic impact, and a number of new objects have been discovered, among them the comets Hyakutake and Hale-Bopp.

Our ability to detect objects like these is primitive. Hyakutake, for example, was only discovered in January of 1996. By April, it was making a spectacular flyby at 10 million miles.

Hale-Bopp is a much larger object, but it seems no more likely to hit us than Hyakutake. At present it is believed that Hale-Bopp is even larger than the great comet of 1811, which lit up night like day. There is no evidence, however, that Hale-Bopp will pose any kind of threat to Earth at all.

It could be that the zodiacal warnings are not about a specific object, but a period of time in which many objects appear. Hale-Bopp and Hyakutake were not predicted. Both 1996 JA-1 and the other near-miss asteroid mentioned previously appeared so unexpectedly that this comment about them had to be added after *The Secret School* had already been delivered to the publisher as complete. They lend additional credibility to this seemingly far-fetched notion.

What is extremely clear is that the old calendars as well as the heavens should be studied carefully, and right now. If we are entering some sort of debris field, it is obviously imperative that we determine this.

What do we know already?

Unfortunately, not as much as we need to. We believe that comets emerge from vast debris clouds that surround the outer solar system, but we know little about these clouds and how they function. Could it actually be that the sudden increase in cometary and asteroidal activity in the solar system is indeed part of a very long cycle, one that was once known to the creators of the long-count calendars? If so, that could be why so many of the long-count calendars based on the zodiac end during our era. In its dying, did the past attempt to warn us that Hamlet's Mill will go berserk again? Given the dating of the calendars and what is being observed right now in the sky, it would be foolhardy to discount this possibility. It is time to abandon old ways of thinking and hidebound scientific disciplines that may be literally jeopardizing our lives by their adherence to theories that ignore what is observably happening in the real world.

The idea that there might have been a civilization sophisticated enough to make such predictions that died before recorded history even began is absolute anathema to modern archaeology, just like the notion of earlier dating for man is to paleontology. And yet, in the spring of 1996, a whole series of stunning redatings have occurred. Peking man has been found to be far older than thought. Tools have been found in Zaire that are the equal of objects created in Europe 30,000 years ago—but the Zairian fossils are 90,000 years old. These dates are not in scientific dispute. Certainly one thing has become clear: man has possessed a high level of toolmaking skill and the social organization that it implies for much longer than was previously thought.

Even so, it is a long stretch to believe that a *civilization* might have existed before the rise of Sumeria and Egypt about five thousand B.C. The reason for this is that a reasonably continuous record of human development can be identified, without significant breaks, that becomes gradually more sophisticated until cities and civilization appear in India, Egypt, and Sumeria, all within about five hundred years of each other.

So where are the remains of the ancient civilization, where were its machines and its great structures, its vast, teeming cities, its writings? Actually, they may be all around us, unrecognized for their true significance. The world is littered with unexplained artifacts that archaeologists and paleontologists simply ignore, or dismiss without serious study because they cannot be explained by accepted theories.

Among these ignored artifacts are cement cylinders found in New Caledonia in 1967 by L. Chevalier of the Museum of New Caledonia. They are very hard, and have been roughly carbon-dated to 5,120–10,950 B.C. Even the earliest date is thousands of years before man is believed to have reached the South Pacific. What's more, the first lime-mortar cement does not appear, according to conventional archaeology, until about 200 B.C.

The cylinders were not imported. The tumuli where they were cast have also been found, seventeen or more on New Caledonia and four hundred on the nearby Isle of Pines. What the cylinders might have been used for, or who made them, remains a complete mystery.

There are dozens of similar mysteries. Some of the strangest artifacts date from much further back. For example, a piece of limestone containing human footprints was found in 1822 near St. Louis. The prints, very detailed and ten and a half inches long, had apparently been impressed when the stone was still soft. This would make them millions of years old—impossibly old, old beyond understanding.

There are some very strange footprints that seem human that were found in a Cretaceous stone near Glen Rose, Texas, in a strata that also contains dinosaur footprints.

In his delightful book *Ancient Man: A Handbook of Puzzling Artifacts*, in which I found many of these stories, noted science writer William Corliss says,

"Entombed toads and man-made spoons found in coal must all be rejected to avoid time paradoxes. Like UFOs and sea monsters, these contrary, seemingly trivial observations keep recurring. The incredible number of such incredibilities make one wonder if we are missing something."

There are also technological objects littering the past, and some of them are very hard to explain. In both Egypt and Peru there have been found small devices that appear to model flying craft. The Egyptian object is dated to 200 B.C., and was found in a tomb at Saqqâra. It is a small carving of a bird fashioned out of sycamore. The interesting thing about it is that the wing has a dihedral, like a modern wing. Not until the Wright brothers flew did the modern world realize the value of this concept. The little Egyptian glider flies beautifully. But who built it? Who knew about the dihedral wing in the Egypt of the pharaohs?

A pre-Incan culture produced a small amulet that appears like a delta-winged aircraft with a vertical rudder and two horizontal stabilizers. It has been assumed to represent a bird or butterfly, but again there is no creature in nature with wings and a tail like that. The only things with such tails are airplanes. There is even an apparent "cockpit." The Hebrew letter *beth* appears on one of the wings, in the place where an insignia would be. However, there is certainly no evidence that any Hebrews were flying around in jets in 500 A.D. when the object was produced, let alone doing it in South America.

At Dendera in Egypt, there exist carvings of objects that have been identified by engineers as looking very much like Crookes tubes, which are forerunners to the cathode ray tube used in television. In the carvings, people are shown sitting under the tubes with their arms extended, as if receiving some sort of blessing or energy from them.

In 1900 a complicated geared device was found off the Greek island of Antikythera, in the debris of a ship that had sunk in 50 B.C. It was discovered to be an astronomical calculator that could be used to determine planetary movements. What is strange about it is that it exhibits a level of gear construction that was not achieved again until the latter part of the seventeenth century. It is the only such object found from the ancient world.

A construction made of iron disks at New Delhi in India, known as the Ashoka Pillar, is at least fifteen hundred years old, and yet has not rusted away. Why not? There is something unknown about the construction technique that was used that prevents it from rusting, and so far no studies have revealed the answer.

The famous crystal skull discovered by F. A. Mitchell in the Mayan city of Lubaantum in Belize would have taken three hundred years of unending work to create using the only known method, which would have involved slow abrasion of the crystal with sand. Otherwise, the technology involved must also be unknown.

At the town of Ica in Peru, there are 20,000 stones of various sizes carved with what appear to be scenes of extraordinary surgical procedures. Many of the carvings are quite exact, and seem to show things like blood transfusions and cesarean sections, tumor excisions and even brain surgery, and the presence of needles at the body sites where acupuncture needles would now be used to reduce pain. These carvings have been in the historical record since the sixteenth century, and are of unknown age. They are certainly from before a time when any of these operations were being done, especially brain surgery.

There are even apparent technological artifacts in much, much older strata, which are really very difficult to explain short of fossil-era astronauts or time travelers.

If the emerging possibility of physical time travel proves true, their existence may perhaps become more understandable. In fact, we may live to see some of them being left behind given the increasing indications from theoretical physics that we are not all that far from achieving the capability to move through time. So far, though, nothing has been found that points to our era—no camcorder lenses or 7UP cans in the Devonian . . . yet.

The list of really old artifacts is also long. Among some interesting examples are a nail that was found embedded in a block of sandstone in England in 1844. The stone was at least 20 million years old, and possibly much older.

In 1852, blasting in Dorchester uncovered a bell-shaped metal vessel decorated with images of flowers inlaid in silver. Nobody knows how this obviously man-made object came to be deeply embedded in stone millions of years old.

An iron cup was found embedded in coal over 100 million years old deep in a mine in Oklahoma. In Illinois, a metal sphere with grooves on it was taken from a Precambrian deposit over 200 million years old, and a gold chain was discovered in similarly ancient coal.

These latter finds, as well as numerous others, date from before the tremendous impact that closed the Permian, and other strange objects have been located in strata that has remained untouched since before life even existed.

Hundreds of metallic spheres of two types, one a hollow ball with a white, spongy center and the other of solid bluish metal, have been found in the Western Transvaal in South Africa. Some have parallel rings carved around their circumferences. In their fascinating book *The Hidden History of the Human Race*, Michael A. Cremo and Richard Thompson comment that the spheres are so hard that they cannot be scratched by steel, and are found in deposits 2.8 billion years old. "In the absence of a satisfactory natural explanation," the authors comment, "the evidence is somewhat mysterious, leaving open the possibility that the South African grooved sphere . . . was made by an intelligent being." One of these extremely mysterious objects, it has been discovered by the curator of the Klerksdorp Museum in South Africa where it is on display, slowly rotates on its own axis even though it is sealed in a display case.

Whatever was happening in the deep past, one thing is certain: the existence of even one such unexplained artifact—and there are many—means that something essential is missing from our theories of the past.

In addition to all these artifacts, there is also a remarkable pattern seen in ancient ruins across this planet: the oldest structures are among the largest and most perfectly built of all structures. Some of them could not be built today at all, because we do not possess equipment capable of moving or working their stones.

The great fortress at Sacsayhuaman, high in the Peruvian Andes, contains stones weighing upwards of 400 tons. The remarkable and profoundly ancient platform at Baalbek in Lebanon, on which a more recent Temple of Jupiter is built, contains blocks weighing upwards of 750 tons, and probably as much as 1,100 tons. The 228-foot-high Black Pagoda in India bears a stone weighing 1,000 tons that has been somehow raised into place.

None of these stones could be handled at the present time with anything approaching the skill with which they were manipulated in the past, and they are not the most telling evidence of the presence of an earlier civilization on Earth.

Nobody knows the age of the Sphinx. There are those who claim that it is far older than the four thousand years attributed to it by conventional thinking. They have interesting reasons. First, it has been weathered, according to geologists, by the action of water, not wind. This fact is revealed by the condition of its sandstone body. According to John Anthony West, it must have been built long before the time of the pharaohs because it shows evidence of water erosion. Dr. Robert Schoch, a Boston University geologist, has confirmed the validity of this theory, and his dating was endorsed by three hundred other geologists at the 1992 convention of the Geological Society of America.

During the time of the pharaohs, Egypt was largely a desert, as it is now. Through all of recorded history, there has not been enough rainfall to explain the water weathering on the Sphinx. However, the past climate of Egypt has been studied carefully, and we know that there was an era when there were extensive rains. They occurred between seven thousand and ten thousand B.C., and would certainly have been capable of producing the weathering seen on this structure. These rains followed the period of extreme upheaval that marked the Age of Leo.

This would mean that the Sphinx was built during a time when civilization in Egypt had barely entered the Age of Agriculture. There were no cities, no kings, no big social groupings, and not even very many people.

So who built it and other Egyptian monuments like the Osireion, another ancient structure that may date from before known history? The Osireion is an enigmatic building in the desert near Abydos. It is the oldest stone building in Egypt, a substantial oblong structure designed to draw groundwater into its seventeen internal pools. It is conventionally dated as being from the era of the Pharaoh Seti I, from a few inscriptions on the otherwise uncarved surfaces of the structure. However, pharaohs were in the habit of claiming structures by inscribing their names on them, so this is no proof of date.

It is interesting to note that there may be a way to actually date the Sphinx that strongly suggests the great antiquity favored by geologists. In the year 10,450 B.C., and in no other year since, the constellation Leo rose precisely behind the body of the

Sphinx, in exact conformity with its shape. This was also the year in which the Sun in the vernal equinox first rose in Leo.

Was the Sphinx a monument commemorating an age, built by sophisticated and capable people who have entirely disappeared? If so, this tradition was continued into later eras. For example, the Temple of Karnak in Luxor, with its famous ram motifs, was built at the beginning of the Age of Aries the Ram. The Old Testament, written during Aries, is filled with references to the ram. By contrast, the gospels are full of references to the fish, and Christ was called "the fisher of men." He was born at the beginning of the Age of Pisces, and is still identified by the symbol of the fish.

Now, as the Age of Aquarius is beginning, it appears that we have lost this ancient tradition, along with most of our other connections to deep human tradition and our real past. Of course, the absence of memory is perhaps appropriate to our formless new sign.

The pyramids at Giza present another bizarre calendrical anomaly. According to engineer Robert Bauval in his book *The Orion Mystery*, the Giza monuments mirror the shape of the constellation of Orion as the sun touched the vernal equinox in 10,450 B.C.

We know of nobody in Egypt capable of building either the Sphinx or the pyramids in that remote time. They could not be constructed now without incredible expense and many years of labor, the Great Pyramid perhaps not at all.

We know where the stones for the upper two-thirds

of the pyramid were quarried, and that 2.3 million blocks averaging about two tons each were used to create its inner mass. There is strong reason to believe that they were placed during the time of the pharaohs. Even so, we cannot understand how the work was done—especially how the Egyptians managed to do it in the twenty years Egyptologists usually estimate as the time needed to build the pyramid, working, as they are supposed to have done, only during seasons when the fields were fallow.

As Graham Hancock points out in his ground-breaking book *Fingerprints of the Gods*, simple math reveals that if 2.3 million stones are to be put in place in twenty years, one must be placed approximately every 2.9 minutes, 365 days a year, 24 hours a day, for the entire period—an obvious impossibility.

Lacking cranes or even block and tackle, it is hard to see how the historical Egyptians, let alone the simple agriculturists and hunter-gatherers who populated the region in ten thousand B.C., could have managed this. Human labor alone could not have moved that many stones that fast over that period of time. In addition, more people would have been needed to successfully place a stone the weight and size of a large car than could have been gotten around it given the exacting tolerances involved in the actual placements.

Egyptologists claim that the pyramids must have been built using earthen ramps. If so, where is the earth that was dug for this purpose? An enormous mass of soil would have been needed, but no such dig has been found. We have found the quarries from which the stone was taken, but there is no direct evidence that earthen ramps—or any sort of ramps, for that matter—were used.

Another mystery surrounds the use of drills in ancient Egypt. The angle of the cores that were drilled out of the granite sarcophagus in the Great Pyramid indicates that a drill pressure of eight tons must have been used. This is not possible with any drill bit that could have been created from the metals available at the time. In fact, no drills have ever been found in Egypt that could have accomplished this dramatic feat, nor any pictures of such drills, nor the apparatus by which an eight-ton drill pressure was achieved.

Where are these drills? How were they made? Where is the drill press? They have been methodically sought for a hundred years, but never found. It is as if this technologically advanced equipment was taken away.

Without clear answers to the questions of engineering and logistics raised by Egyptian monuments and artifacts, we cannot say with certainty that we understand these early structures, either their origins or their manner of construction.

Where did the builders come from? The Egyptians themselves referred to Ta-Neteru, a land of gods to the south, and Egypt was not alone in looking south for such a land. The Mahabharata of ancient India does as well, as does the Popol Vuh from South America.

Even antiquity did not know how its wonders had been built. The pyramids constructed by identified pharaohs are notably less sophisticated than the more enigmatic structures on the Giza plateau. And why is it that the earliest pyramids show the most sophisticated construction techniques? Clearly, skills were being lost as Egypt got older, not gained.

There are ancient structures in South America no less mysterious than the pyramids. How anybody ever transported the immense stones used, for example, in the construction of the Sacsayhuaman fortress up narrow mountain passes to the cliff where it was built is completely unknown.

In his *Royal Commentaries of the Incas and General History of Peru,* the Spanish historian Garcilaso de la Vega tells how an Inca emperor attempted to have a huge boulder brought to the site in the sixteenth century. The project had to be abandoned after 3,000 men died, so even the Incas apparently did not know how it was done.

Until some means of accurately dating the time that stone was worked or carved is found, there is no way to tell the actual age of a structure like Sacsayhuaman, but such a story strongly implies that it must pre-date the Inca culture that thrived from the ninth to the fifteenth centuries.

The trouble is, before the Incas, there simply isn't evidence of any culture capable of such massive building projects. And yet, there is also cultural evidence that some sort of civilized society pre-dated recorded history.

Like the Egyptians and the Hindus, the peoples of the Americas had legends of magicians who came up from the south. The Incas referred to them as Viracocha, he Mayans and Aztecs spoke of Quetzalcoatl. As in all other cases, they came from the sea and the south.

If we even entertain the notion that all of this represents a previous civilization, then what happened to it and why did they build on this incredible scale?

Was there a war in heaven, as ancient Hindu texts suggest, a war that destroyed a great human civilization about twelve thousand years ago? Could it have been with Mars? Or are the Bible, the Popol Vuh, and many other ancient texts correct in describing a great natural catastrophe that involved massive floods and planet-wide dislocations? Was it a catastrophe on a cosmic scale so great that Mars, also, was devastated?

Or could both things be true? Certainly, it is beyond serious dispute that there was a catastrophe on this planet about twelve thousand years ago. The remains of this catastrophe are plain to see in the geologic record. They include the bodies of thousands of large mammals all across the arctic circle, quick-frozen with food still in their mouths, grasses frozen in the tender of spring, trees frozen with buds still intact on their boughs.

In China and Mongolia, there are ridges of bones that contain the tusks of uncounted masses of these animals. Across the whole northern hemisphere, and especially in the Americas, large animal species went extinct at about this time. Some of this can probably be accounted for by the action of hunters, but what can account for piles of skeletons so huge that they were mined for their ivory by the historical Chinese? About the only thing that could have done that would have been massive tidal waves.

Something terrible happened on this earth around ten thousand B.C. Although it offers no dating, the

Popol Vuh describes the sun as shooting into the southern sky like a meteor, as if the Earth itself was tumbling wildly in its orbit, and then a period of "forty years" of darkness during which people suffered greatly and civilization fell.

In fact, hardly a single ancient text fails to describe this disaster. From the Sumerian Epic of Gilgamesh to the Bible to the Vedantic texts of India to the Popol Vuh, there is description after description of a huge worldwide catastrophe.

There are also some more subtle indicators. Among the Aztecs, there was a legend that the great pyramid complex of Teotihuacan was built by the gods during a day when the sun never came up. Interestingly, the Bible mentions a day—on the opposite side of the Earth—when the sun never went down (Joshua 10:12–13). This certainly suggests a real event of some kind, although what might have stopped the planet's rotation without destroying everything that wasn't firmly attached to its surface is difficult to imagine.

Did a heavenly body pass through our solar system, disrupting Earth? And what happened to Mars? If the artifacts—the face, the pyramids, the ruined walls—that appear in the Viking photographs really are artifacts, why are they in ruins?

In the ancient Indian Vedas, mankind is described as having the ability to "fly on the winds" and to create things like sonar-guided rockets and massive "cities" in the sky. Where did these men go? How could primitive Hindu poets possibly have conceived of esoteric military technology and flying machines?

In *Fingerprints of the Gods,* Hancock discusses the

theory that the civilization that we have called Atlantis since the time of the Greek philosopher Plato, who first described it and said that it had suffered inundation, was situated in the Antarctic. His concept is based on a book by Roger and Rose Flem-Ath, *When the Sky Fell*.

The idea is drawn, in part, from an examination of a group of medieval maps that show the outlines of the Antarctic coastline as it was before it became covered with ice. One of the earliest of these maps, the indisputably genuine Oronteus Finaeus map of 1531, reveals an accurate outline of the subglacial features of Queen Maud Land, Enderby Land, Wilkes Land, Victoria Land, and Marie Byrd Land on the Antarctic continent. These sub-ice structures could not have been mapped at any time in recorded history, because this area of the Antarctic has been covered with ice for the past six thousand years. It was not until 1949 that a seismic survey of Queen Maud Land confirmed the stunning accuracy of the ancient maps.

Even if some of these maps are actually from later dates, as has been suggested, nobody claims, or could ever claim, that they were created after 1949. Both the Piri Reis and Oronteus Finaeus maps are documented as having existed before that date. So who could have known, prior to that year, what the Antarctic continent looked like under its miles-thick ice cover?

The Oronteus Finaeus map was, according to Dr. Richard Strachan of the Massachusetts Institute of Technology, devised using earlier source maps that combined a number of different projection techniques. Nobody knows the origin of the Piri Reis map, but it also seems to be a copy of an earlier effort that was apparently in the library of the Imperial Palace at Constantinople, where Reis allegedly copied it.

Was there a highly developed civilization in Antarctica in the distant past? If so, what happened to it? Where did the water I saw in my vision come from, what was the origin of the vast geologic catastrophe that took place, and why did the leaders of that now-defunct civilization go to places like Egypt and leave enigmatic monuments that seem intended to last for eternity?

It is time to decode the hidden meaning of the pyramids and understand the message of the Sphinx. It is time to stop snickering about the zodiac and accept the idea that there exists on this planet a stellar calendar of immense antiquity and sophistication.

An ancient world left a warning, it would appear, intended to save the people of a distant age from a repeat of the catastrophe that befell them. Ours is that age, I believe, and we are the people for whom that warning was intended.

The Future

THE LAST LESSON IN THE SUMMER OF MY NINTH YEAR was of a very different kind. I had entered the ice of the past, and now it was time to use the skills I had gained to go into the future.

But for the occasional thunderstorm, the drought-ridden summer of 1954 was composed of a long string of agonizingly hot days, evenings swept by dry breezes, and nights so still that whispers echoed. And there in the deep night is the little boy. He is asleep now. The spotted dog sits guard at the foot of the bed. Over this summer, which for her has been a long one, her eyes have become rimmed by premature gray.

It seems impossible that so much could have been happening in the subtext of a child's life, especially in that peaceful, deeply settled world. But human experience is many layered, and there are certainly levels that we do not acknowledge.

I am drawn to the simplicity of most of the memories

that identify those days in my mind: my father's shadow lingering in the doorway, my scuffed shoes beside the bed, my child's desk stacked with books about Egypt and Rome and the stars. Using these images as anchors, I search deeper, going closer to the sleeping child, finding him in my mind's eye, retrieving the flavor of his life, evoking the little boy who sleeps within me now, who once rode the shoulders of the night.

I was a yearning child in a summer of mysteries, the most extraordinary of which was just about to unfold. It had become a summer of obsessions and the latest was Rome. I could see Roman faces and walk in Roman streets. I could perceive a Roman life unfolding as a kind of superimposition on the trees and bicycles and movies of ordinary days. The people of Rome became as real to me as my own friends and family. I bought *Augustus Caesar's World* by Genevieve Foster, and spent hours dreaming about the life of the young Octavius.

Normally, I was an active, outgoing child, but there were times of deep reflection that summer. I can remember whole afternoons on the roof by myself, watching the sky and listening to the wind in the trees, and imagining that when I opened my eyes I would be in Rome, or on Mars, or in the timeless long-ago.

I dreamed of comets and the rolling earth, and awoke in tears. I became desperate to find fossils, and managed to get the father of my neighbor, who was a geologist, to take us fossil hunting. I found a piece of conglomerate full of shells and spent hours worrying them out of the mass. I wanted a fossil trilobite. I speculated that sow bugs had descended from trilobites. I wondered if trilobites were edible.

I thought of the Sister of Mercy as real, and assumed that she was a genuine nun. If she wasn't, then the setting of the secret school near an old nun's home was a clever deception, designed to create an impression that would cause us to automatically respond to her as an authority figure.

When I asked my mother about the Sisters of Mercy, she said that the order didn't exist. To my surprise, I was sharply forbidden to mention it again. It was only later that I discovered that "Sister of Mercy" was a euphemism for prostitute. That was the last conversation I had with anybody about those particular nuns.

I had the constant feeling that I had lost something, or that I was myself lost. San Antonio wasn't my real home, I decided. I was a time traveler from ancient Rome, I decided. To our priests' amazement, my Latin began to improve at mass. I had begun to study seriously so that I would be ready when it was time to go home. During the day, I lived out a fantasy life in Rome that mirrored the one I remembered at night. I thought a great deal about Octavius.

I also began to search through history books looking for the other civilization I had seen, again without consciously knowing why. My method was to borrow my grandfather's high school text, *Ancient History* by Philip Van Ness Myers, and read it page by careful page.

I found it among my mother's things and have it here with me now, lying in my hands. Scratched in pencil in the frontispiece is a name, "Alice Richards,

Poteet, Texas." I can remember how I wondered about Alice Richards, who she may have been and why we got the book from her. Back then, Mother had explained to me that I would find nothing there about the antediluvian world, but I read it anyway.

I added time travel to the repertoire of games I had invented. One afternoon we might fly to Mars, the next to ancient Rome or Egypt, or the world before the flood. I built a time machine helmet out of my football helmet, some wire, and some thread spools. I found it hard to believe that it would not work. Two years later, I would try to build an anti-gravity drive and blow out our electricity. I do not yet remember what inspired me to try to construct such a thing, but it must have had something to do with the lessons of other summers.

I began attending Mrs. Carter's regular astronomy class, which had been extended into August. Lessons were given at the Witte Museum, with Friday-night trips to her observatory.

When I finally got to go there officially, I was eager to see the telescope. When it came time for me to look through it, I stood up on a little bench and peered into the brass eyepiece. Immediately, I saw the colliding galaxies. My voice full of excitement, I reported this to Mrs. Carter.

She looked—and, of course, did not see any such thing. Any colliding galaxies were much too far away to be discerned by her telescope as much more than a smudge.

"They have this Milky Way in their sky that looks like it's on fire. But it's sad there. The people are real quiet because they know that their world is ending."

She gave me a brief hug as I came down from the

step. I do not remember if she said anything. I remember well, though, that she moved the 'scope and found Mars.

As I waited my turn, I was beside myself with excitement. Finally I got to the step and peered into the eyepiece. "I see the Sphinx," I yelled. "I went there with these nuns," I jabbered. "There are nuns living on Mars. They live in a great big mountain."

This created something of a stir, as the other boys also wanted to see these objects on Mars. Finally, Mrs. Carter sent me down into the "ballroom" to wait until the class was over. I ended up discovering some toy cars, and spent the half hour it took for Mother to come get me playing with them.

I remember nothing about the journey home, except that we listened to a ballad on Mother's favorite station, KITE radio, and not much was said. A few days later, however, I was taken out to Our Lady of the Lake University and given an extensive series of mental tests by Mother's friend Dr. Wren. I do not believe that the tests revealed any abnormality, as there was no follow-up. Six years later, when my brother was four, he was also taken for these tests.

The end of August came, but the sun stayed cruel. If a drought as severe as that one struck now, South Texas would run out of water. To escape the heat, we went to my grandparents' house in the hill country north of San Antonio.

One stifling night I stepped out onto the upstairs porch. I had once been so frightened of the dark that I wouldn't have gone even this far outside on my own, but not now.

I walked along the porch, which went around two sides of the house. The moon was high, and I sang, "I see the moon, the moon sees me . . ."

After a time, I realized that there was something odd in the sky above the live oak tree that overhung this end of the porch. This is something I have never really forgotten, although I must admit that it receded in importance as I matured.

Although I recalled the initial sighting, I remembered nothing of what happened later that night. When I was a teenager, I would take many pictures of that tree, trying in some way to reconcile myself to the appalling recollections that had been deposited in my unconscious.

Over Thanksgiving of 1995, I went to the house again. It is much the same as it was in those days, and the old tree still overhangs the porch. I stood precisely in the place I had stood on that night in 1954, and looked up into the empty autumn sky. I laid my hand on the porch rail, just where I had put it that night. I had stood here for some time, I remembered, looking up at the object. I could see my mother, who was smoking and reading on the big bed in my grandparents' room. Candy and Mom's cocker Sidney were on the bed with her.

I kept looking from that reassuring scene to the fantastic apparition above the house. The thing was like a glowing cutout pasted against the darkness, it was so flat and motionless. I said to my mother, "I see a flying saucer."

"It's time for you to come in."

"Come see it."

"It's bedtime, Whitty."

I obeyed her, deciding, I suppose, that it must be something else. That was the end of the flying saucer, but not of the journeys of that night. I had been put in a small bedroom that I liked very much on the front corner of the house, except that on this particular night it was really hot. It had a radio, and I loved listening. At night, you might pick up stations from anywhere, and I enjoyed imagining the signals sailing across the dark.

In my shower, I pretended that I was a saucer pilot, and we went to the colliding galaxies to save everybody. Mom tucked me and Candy in and we said a Hail Mary together. For the moment, the flying saucer was forgotten. Mother read aloud from Carl Sandburg's autobiography, which was the book she'd been reading in bed. Afterward, I read *Augustus Caesar's World* until I got drowsy. Along with *The Glory of Egypt* by Michel Audrain, bought the next year, and *Never to Die: The Egyptians in Their Own Words,* by Josephine Mayer and Tom Prideaux, this book is the only possession I still retain from those years. These three books, which have stayed with me always, were also the closest things to textbooks that I had in the secret school.

Without knowing why, I have placed enormous value on them all of my life. Except for the rosary my grandfather gave me, I have not one other thing from childhood.

When the lights were out and it was just me and Candy, my mind returned to that strange device I'd seen in the sky. I wanted to go back out on the porch and find out if it was still there. My fear fought with my curiosity. As has been the case throughout my life, curiosity won.

I went through the window-door that led from my room to the porch. The night was magnificent, but I couldn't see anything unusual. I looked across the broad view of the Texas hills. There was nothing but the purple sky and the stars.

Then I saw three shadows down in the yard. At first I thought they were little hooded people, but then I had the feeling that they were animals, maybe coyotes.

They disturbed me and I went back inside. I turned my radio on low, to enjoy the comfort of voices and music and the security of the yellow-lighted dial. Then I heard the front door close, very softly. I called, "Mom," but there was no answer. Silence settled in again.

I was shocked a few moments later to hear the clock downstairs strike three. I sat up, confused. Had I counted the strikes correctly? The concept of missing time was not available to me, so I was completely mystified. Half the night had somehow passed.

I was moving to turn off the radio when I saw a hooded shape in my doorway. As I stared, it seemed to drift back away from me with the movement of my eyes, but I was not deceived. I'd seen that before. I sat up. "Hi," I whispered.

Then it was day. It shocked the very devil out of me and I cried out. I remember that it felt like an explosion, such was the suddenness with which the light appeared, streaming in the windows.

I ran to the window-door and stared out, stunned by the sunny view. Three airplanes were flying south to north. They were noisy, and looked to me like fighters of some sort, with wing pods and a triangular configuration. "Look at the planes," I yelled into the thunder of their passing. Nobody reacted. The silence they left behind was very deep.

The farms down in the valley—thriving, as far as I knew—were all overgrown. As I remember, I can clearly feel the shock that went through me when I saw that. Every summer evening here for all of my life, I had listened to the farm wife calling in the cows and the tinkling of their bells. Nobody would be calling cows down there again, that was obvious.

I also noticed that the trees near our house were gray and dead. The drought was causing a lot of trees to die, but this did not make sense. Just that afternoon, our trees had been fine.

I crept down the porch, wishing that the sun wasn't so bright, trying to figure out what was going on. I noticed that the color of the sky was strange. It was purple-blue, not the pure, sweet blue that I had always known. The light of the sun was knife-sharp.

I reached out and touched a branch of the tree that overhung the porch. It was covered with a kind of gray crust. As a boy, I loved to climb trees, and certain of them I considered personal friends. This was a good friend, and it upset me terribly that it had died. I wanted to tell my mother.

When I went back into the house, I found that my bed was not my bed anymore, it was another bed. The radio was gone and so was the table it had been on. "Candy?" She was nowhere to be seen, and we were always together in those days. "Mom?"

Nobody answered. I listened to the silence, then set out to find everybody.

My mother wasn't in my grandparents' room. Not

only that, it also had a different bed. Hurrying now, I went through her room and back out onto the porch, trying to see if our car was still in the carport. Not only was the car nowhere to be seen, the carport itself was gone. There were other outbuildings. I couldn't see our windmill anymore and the barn was obscured by dead trees and structures I didn't recognize.

I called for my mother and my father but there was only silence in reply. I ran downstairs, across the familiar broad landing and into the living room. The room was still the same shape and color, but the furniture was different. The brass lettered lines from Browning's "Pippa Passes," GOD'S IN HIS HEAVEN: ALL'S RIGHT WITH THE WORLD, still stood over the passageway between the living and dining rooms, along with the picture of Our Lady of Guadalupe that had been there since the house was built.

Then I saw a television, which was on. As far as I knew, there was no TV in the house, and I was very pleased to see this one. I stared at it in astonishment, though, because the picture was not only in color, it was amazingly beautiful. The set was flat, about the thickness of a book, standing on a low table. The jewel-like picture delighted me.

The scenes I saw on that television remained in my mind all of my life—not exactly as a conscious memory, but rather as a reservoir of visual images that I have come to draw on in my work. They have figured in a number of my books, especially as the inspiration for many of the scenes in *Nature's End*.

On the TV, I saw a very white-faced man talking. He was wearing a black suit. He talked in short bursts. I do not consciously remember much of what he said, but the images are clear. There was a weather report that used multileveled and multicolored maps seen from above. Obviously it was an advanced version of a satellite weather map. At the time, I had no idea what it was. Only as the years passed did its meaning become more clear to me. Like a number of other images from the secret school, it recurred in my mind as an extremely vivid memory during the height of my early encounter experiences. At that time, I reported it as a multilayered weather map. At the time, I thought it was something new, though, placed in my mind by some mysterious process of telepathy.

There was a box in one corner of the screen that showed an image of the sun and had a row of numbers beneath it. I then saw the image of an airplane that I later recognized as a Boeing 747 jumbo jet from its distinctive shape and huge size.

A bell was tolling, and the fact that the plane was parked on a runway half-covered with sand made me assume, in 1954, that I was looking at something on Mars. The plane was blue and white, and I think now that what I heard being announced was that it was *Air Force One*, which had been grounded at Los Angeles Airport because of a sandstorm. This sand-bound plane became one of the key images in the as-yet-unproduced film script of *Above Top Secret*, my movie about the Roswell Incident, the alleged crash of a UFO near Roswell, New Mexico, in 1947.

I saw images of sand dunes blowing across an abandoned playground. There were also pictures of doctors in what looked like the crowded ward of a slum hospital. I recall being confused by all the machinery. The people on the beds looked like they were parts of a scientific experiment, there was so much equipment. Everybody looked human, but wasn't this Mars?

I sat down in front of the TV. I had decided that it was a real interociter, as in the film, and my main hope was that they wouldn't take it away. I saw huge clouds rising, it seemed, all the way to space. My sense of this was that it was smoke coming up from some kind of vast fire.

This was not the only fire I saw. There were others, many fires. There were shots of whole cities under clouds of smoke. I saw fire race through a beautiful neighborhood, so vividly real that I screamed and ran to the far side of the room.

The whole TV program unfolded with a choppy delivery that I could hardly follow. Everything was faster, everything was louder, the color amazed me.

I saw columns of people walking down roads in a scruffy landscape, columns that went on forever and ever. These people were Oriental in appearance. There were many others lying on the roadside. This was China, and ever since that day I have been waiting for a grave catastrophe involving mass migration to strike that country.

There was a scene in a city that might have been European. There were thousands of people, it seemed to me, lying everywhere. Everything was a mess, and there seemed to be an awful lot of dead.

In another scene, set over what was clearly Manhattan, a huge object, cigar-shaped and lighted with bright red lights, came down as if through a slit in the sky, making a crackling sound. A highway with all the cars abandoned became a scene in my nuclear winter novel, *Wolf of Shadows*.

I saw children playing on a patio. They had floppy clothes on and black helmets that reminded me of the ones we wore in the secret school. These kids had dolls that looked like the Sisters of Mercy. They were moving their arms very quickly and singing in shrill voices. I found this incredibly alarming, and was glad when the scene changed.

There were scenes of the pyramids and a man talking very excitedly. He wore a big hat and dark glasses that covered half of his face. The thing that surprised me was that the pyramids were in the middle of a city, and it looked like a dead city to me. Cairo, of course, is now reaching the Giza Plateau and will completely surround it in a very few years.

The man talking was in a group of people. I was fascinated with them, chiefly with all the equipment that everybody seemed to possess. They carried little cases. They all had hats and dark glasses and were manipulating small machines that they pointed here and there. Looking back, I think that these may have been video cameras, unknown to me then.

I then saw a sequence that, like the fires, has remained with me as a kind of internal emblem. It started with a huge iron disc standing in the middle of black space. This was vibrating and there was a noise associated with it, the great bell tolling that was also associated with the image of the 747 trapped in the sand, and the sense of urgency reminded me of the ticking that had started my summer.

With each enormous clang, the iron ball vibrated. Then it became covered with dark hills and valleys and mountains, then a layer of glowing material, then the familiar continents and seas. You could still see across all the layers, though, down to the original iron. There was a numbered scale floating in this animated, three-dimensional map, and with each clang all the continents went into motion. Their edges folded into the oceans, mountains rose and flattened, and the position of the polar caps changed.

I understood that this was the Earth, but I did not know the significance of what I was seeing. I stared, not comprehending, and I still don't understand, unless it was depicting some sort of slippage between the Earth's crust and its deeper layers.

I walked away, drawn by other needs. I was hungry and wanted my breakfast. I went toward the kitchen, but was stopped in my tracks before I got there by something I found in the pantry.

My grandparents' familiar white fridge was gone, and in its place was a black thing with a clear glass door. I walked up to it and looked in. It was a refrigerator unlike any I had ever seen before. You didn't even need to open it to find out what you had. I did open it, though. I wanted some ham. We'd brought a big ham up with us.

As I leaned into the coolness, I felt a loneliness so powerful that it was almost organic. Lurching back, I screamed for my mother. I ran out onto the back porch. Everything in the house pasture appeared to be dead, the trees, the shrubs. Even the ground was naked.

I dashed around the side of the house to the front porch, climbed the steps, and ran past dark green Adirondack chairs, not the white ones we had.

Skidding around the corner, nearly blind with panic, I was caught short by the appearance of a figure at the far end of the long porch. He had just come out of the door that leads from the kitchen. He was wearing khaki pants and a puffy white shirt. He had on a hat and dark glasses. He raised his hand and spoke in a dry old voice: "Stop, son. Stop now."

The feelings that came to me when I heard his voice were overwhelmingly powerful. They were feelings of love, vast, electrifying, far greater than any I had known before. The impulse to go to him was almost impossible to resist, and I suppose that I kept running, because he cried out, "No!"

I stopped. He sounded so familiar, this dry old man. So familiar! Remembering it, I am almost overwhelmed with the power of the thing again. The love was appalling.

I would swear that this happened, on pain of death. So please try to stay with me, at least a little, when I tell you that when that old man took off his big dark glasses, I knew immediately that he was me. I could see it in his face, I could feel it in my heart, in every cell of my being.

I could feel him moving when I moved, breathing as I breathed, could feel the way his insides felt. He breathed with me, and when I moved, he also moved. Between us was a living, shimmering presence—our reality, our mutuality of self, unbound by time, in total communion with the miraculous mystery of being.

He said something and I felt my own chest flutter, my own vocal chords vibrate. He said, "Tell your sister . . ." I ended the sentence for him: ". . . that I love her."

In those days, actually saying something like that would have been the equivalent of unconditional surrender. I admired my sister, who was bigger, stronger, and smarter—or at least better informed. However, she was a girl.

As the years have passed, though, the love of those days has been buried, and what ought to have become a dear old companionship has never happened. How odd that the most telling—and, to me, most important—message back from that dying, immensely accomplished world would be something so personal.

I don't remember very well the return to 1954. It was night again, though, and I was back in my bedroom, a shocked and amazed little boy, a frightened little boy, left to tremble in the dark. I longed to see my mother and sister, but I still thought that they were gone. It did not occur to me to try to find them in the house.

Confused as I was, I was also a very tired nine-year-old. As I drifted off to sleep, a choir of gentle voices sang the old ballad "On Top of Old Smoky."

And so my summer in the secret school ended, although I did not know it at the time, of course. A few days after this incident, the family returned to San Antonio, which remained as hot as ever.

I was taken down to Frank Brothers men's store and fitted for my new school uniforms, a ritual that, for me, was the most certain signal that summer was at an end. Without understanding why, I began to feel an emptiness inside.

Even though the conscious awareness of my secret life had been buried, I still missed it. I enjoyed school and usually looked forward to going back, but this summer was different. The closer ordinary school came, the more lonely I felt.

I began to pretend that I had friends who were spacemen. We went on adventures together. We went to Mars, then to Metaluna, the planet from *This Island Earth*. I decided that Metaluna was real. I prayed for Exter, the head of the Metalunans, to come down and save me from being a mere fourth grader.

I embarked on secret expeditions to track the Metalunans down. I went into the basement and along every bit of crawl space that I knew of in the house. I went out late at night and shone my flashlight up at the sky. I no longer remembered the Olmos Basin.

Inwardly I knew that I wasn't really looking for the Metalunans. Somebody had gone and left me behind. I was alone and I did not want to be here.

I got into the clothes hamper and went to the most secret place in the house, a three-foot area that could only be reached by sitting in the hamper, rocking it closed, and squeezing out over the top. You ended up behind one of my sister's closets. This, I decided, was where the spacemen stayed when they came to the house. I started leaving them notes, but the notes were never picked up.

I knew what they looked like: they were very thin and they wore dark glasses. I begged them to come out of the clothes hamper, but they never did. I swore to them that this time I wouldn't get scared, but it didn't help.

I organized a final sleep-out with a big bonfire in

the secret hope that we would be noticed from above. Nothing happened, not even when I danced around the embers when all the other kids were asleep.

Labor Day came and went, and soon I was on my way to the bus stop each morning, trying not to let the dew ruin the shine on my shoes and get me demerits. Autumn passed into winter, and my sadness built into anger. I had been orphaned, unfairly abandoned. I began to make small painted figures and hide them in corners and under furniture. They were my eyes and ears, they would allow me to see what I was missing from my life.

I got mad at the spacemen. They were mean, I decided. They didn't like me. They were vampires. That Christmas I asked for only one thing: a suit of armor. Somewhere, somehow, my father procured a breastplate, a helmet with a visor, and a sword. I went out Christmas night, raised my sword to the cold, immense sky, and shouted as loud as I could, "Merry Christmas, merry Christmas!" And I thought, I've got armor now, real armor. But I did not have real armor, not against what awaited me, for that was my whole future out there in the dark.

The days of childhood would pass away, and then the days of youth, and those wonderful, mysterious summers would be reduced to snapshots and remembrance. I would grow up and leave Texas, seeking some proof of myself far away. Marriage would come, my own son would be born, and for a few years the laughter of boyhood would once again seem part of me. But he would grow up and go his way as well, and time would flow on.

No armor is proof against that.

COMMENTARY ON THE NINTH LESSON

Prophecy

Why is it that the mind of man is trying so very hard just at present to see into the future? Is it that we fear that we don't have one?

As the zodiac moves from Pisces to Aquarius, other stellar calendars, among them the Mayan and Hopi, predict that there will be a massive and fundamental change—the end of this age—between 2005 and 2012.

Even mathematics may predict great change. At the present rate of increase, by 2010 human knowledge could conceivably be doubling every day. It has been speculated that, in 2012, knowledge will reach the infinite. Modern statistics and ancient calendrical science, it seems, coincide.

People who have had visitor encounters and near-death experiences around the world are suddenly raising their voices in prophecy. In many cases, such as that of Dannion Brinkley, who has had a near-death experience, the prophecies are accurate.

As early as 1983, I was recalling images from my childhood visit to the future, and have documented proof of the accuracy of the prophecies in *Nature's End*.

It would seem that we live in a world that is hanging by a thread, but we also have extraordinary powers that we can bring to bear to save ourselves. The old world, with its old ways of thinking and living, is over. The human population of this planet is too gigantic and too hungry to be effectively controlled.

It may be that the developed countries can enforce the draconian environmental measures that will be necessary in a few years. However, this simply isn't going to happen in the Third World, not unless most countries radically change policies that now encourage open-ended development.

The message of the secret school is that there is an entirely new way to address the situation. We cannot avoid our environmental problems. We cannot avoid the change of the age. But we can reach a new state of mind, a new way of being human, that will enable at least some of us to deal with the crisis in innovative ways that are vastly more effective than what has been accomplished using the old methods.

There are many keys to the door we need to open. The secret school is one of those keys. It teaches that the human mind is much more powerful than we dare let ourselves believe. Because we fear the unknown, we fear our own potential. Most of all, mankind fears mankind.

Strange things keep happening—miracle cures occur, psychics read minds, prophets correctly foretell the future. The list is long. We deny and deride and ignore these things, not because they aren't true, but because they are. Instinctively, we are probably aware of the fact that this strange, immensely potent *presence* within us can completely revise reality, and the possibility frightens us.

The secret school is part of the process of revising reality—a clandestine meeting of minds struggling to restitch the fabric of the world. It is about getting free of time, about remembering ourselves in all our truth.

Who founded the secret school—this hidden gateway to the timeless larger mind that is our true self? Was it visitors from some other planet? If so, why lavish all this attention on us? Or was it our own souls, or people from the past or the future, or some other meaning of reality altogether?

Those are not important questions to answer now. What is important to realize is that the secret school was founded by the mind, and it lives in the mind. It is not only a collection of ruined benches in a tattered wilderness area. It is not the private property of a few people who happened to participate in it physically. The secret school is in all of us and belongs to all of us. It is the process of ceasing to be afraid of ourselves and facing what we truly are, of acquiring and learning how to use the power of joy.

The mind is the teacher, also the student. Of all the truths that are emerging out of this strange colloquy, perhaps the greatest is that time itself—even time—may become our servant.

Over history, we have often tried to use the tool of prophecy, but never with any objectivity. In the past, our efforts were obscured by emotionalism and mystical mumbo jumbo. In recent years, this wonderful tool has been debased into sensationalistic trash. We have done this for the same reason that we deny the existence of any and all gateways into the more potent levels of reality: to protect the precious ignorance that gives life the zest and surprise, the wonder and horror, that are capable of changing our souls.

As important as that sort of evolution is, however, it is not more important than life itself. The world I saw as a child is roaring at us like a runaway train.

It does not have to overtake us, though. We have the tools right at hand to change the future. Because we believe that we are helpless, we deny realities we don't want to face by embracing false notions such as "there is no ozone hole" and "global warming doesn't matter." Then there are those who say that nature will "correct itself." These are the ones who speak in terms of a "dieback" of the human species. What can such talk mean to our children?

What if a hundred experts trained in prophecy, working separately under controlled conditions, were able to develop a consistent picture of the climate in, say, fifty years? By acting now, we could cause the future to change, I feel sure. The future would belong to us, if we would only make use of the early warning system that we have been given.

Prophecy is not an excluding grace, either. Well-informed effort can evoke the capacity in almost anybody. Jim Kunetka and I both prophesied effectively during the writing of our 1986 book, *Nature's End*— not because we were special, but because we tried.

Jim's most powerful prophecy was a very exact description of a nuclear accident identical to Chernobyl, written in 1985. It took place in a similar reactor and unfolded in exactly the same way. It was considered so improbable at the time that it was edited out of the published version of *Nature's End*. On April 25, 1986, Chernobyl exploded.

Much of the material in *Nature's End* is extrapolated from things that were known in 1985. However, some of it is pure prophecy. There are trivial matters, such as the name of a Korean-made car that figures in the story, the Hunyadi. The book was written long before the Hyundai was introduced from Korea.

When we were writing *Nature's End*, I was a million miles from remembering what had happened to me in my childhood. In those days, all I had were the recurring dreams of riding my bike into the blackness, but my childhood visions were poured into the book by my unconscious mind.

The first image from the secret school that occurs in *Nature's End* is drawn from the televised picture I saw of thousands of people walking along a road somewhere in Asia. Specifically, the statement "columns of starved, struggling Chinese have been spotted making their way through the Himalayas in a desperate attempt to reach India" that appears on page 55 of the book reflects this part of the vision.

Like everything in the vision, the picture of those people on their death march "stuck" to my conscious mind without any knowledge of where it came from.

At that time, China was just beginning to become a major economic power. It was not anticipated in the mid-eighties that it would become a food importer as its income grew. "Analysts assumed that food production would rise to meet those demands," according to the World Watch Institute.

A child of nine saw desperate Chinese walking down a road in a vision in 1954, and as an adult recorded the vision in a book in 1985. The event seems to happen in the early twenty-first century. If prophecy was an accepted and reliably controlled tool, we would be able to tell how accurate this prediction is and work to change it. As matters stand, whatever is going to happen to the Chinese is simply going to happen. With China importing food right now as world reserves dwindle and food production levels off against a background of increasingly unstable weather, it could well be that this prophecy reveals an extremely serious problem.

When *Nature's End* was being written, the opening of ozone holes was just being discovered and had received little, if any, publicity. One of the characters says, "UV holes kill babies," in reference to a futuristic aircraft tearing such holes in the high atmosphere.

In *Communion*, I warned that there will be "measurable crop damage from excessive ultraviolet light beginning to occur in the 1990–1993 period." In 1995, it was reported that the stomas of plants were becoming smaller because of increased UV radiation caused by the thinning ozone layer. In addition, there must be some reason why plankton is dying in the Western Pacific. Plankton is the basis of the oceanic food chain and a contributor of atmospheric oxygen.

In the chapter of *Nature's End* entitled "Memories," I reconstructed the image of the burning neighborhood I had seen when I was nine. In the book, this terrible fire sweeps through an expensive subdivision in the hills above Los Angeles. At the time it was written, there had never been a fire on such a scale. In 1993, fires swept California in a holocaust that *Time* magazine described as "biblical" in proportion. Twenty-five people were killed in a firestorm in Oakland so close to the fire described in *Nature's End* that the book could have been a news story about an event that took place eight years after it was written.

The book also describes something we called Nonspecific Sclerosing Disease, a mysterious ailment that causes slow death. As it was being published, AIDS was publicly identified.

In many ways, the most interesting things I saw of the future as a child were the various animated maps. Their multileveled complexity suggests a great increase in computer memory and far more sensitive weather detection systems, even given present standards. The most extraordinary of these maps, I think, was one that had not been in my memory at all until the series of contemplations that led to this book. It was the map of the inner earth, which showed the crust sliding along the mantle with amazingly fast repercussions.

It seems that this idea, also, is not without historical precedent and scientific backing. Professor Charles H. Hapgood, author of *Earth's Shifting Crust: A Key to Some Basic Problems of Earth Science* (Pantheon, 1958), has proposed that just this process may account for the seeming suddenness with which certain types of change have taken place in the past. Judging from the fact that mammoths are found in Alaska and Siberia that were literally quick-frozen, the crustal movement must be very rapid.

I wonder, then, if the image on the television screen might not have been an illustration of this process from a time in the future when they know and understand that it is going to happen. If so, then maybe the catastrophe that took place during the Age of Leo had another dimension to it, in the sense that something—perhaps an impact—set up a vibration that led to crustal shift. If the core is crystalline, it could be that powerful vibrations could develop even after a relatively minor impact.

Such a thing would drag the crust along the sub-surface of the planet, causing extraordinary upheavals and leaving a dust cloud that would persist for decades—or, as the Popol Vuh described it, "forty years of darkness."

Had this happened when I went into the future, what I would have seen, if anything, would have been ruins in murky darkness, but the world was intact and the sun was shining with notable ferocity.

The problem with the idea that the lithosphere, or outer layer of the planet, periodically shifts is similar to the one with the notion of a lost civilization. Just as there is strong evidence that all people known to have been in the world in ten thousand B.C. were primitive hunter-gatherers and subsistence farmers, there is a clear geologic record over most of the world during the same period, and it doesn't seem to include anything so dramatic as a crustal shift.

Interestingly, though, one area where there are extensive undated ruins is also an area where it is apparent that dramatic geologic changes have taken place, quite possibly as recently as ten thousand B.C. This area is South America. Not only does the Popol Vuh record a calamity, by far the most extensive mysterious ruins are in the area of the Andes. There is evidence that a dramatic rise in the elevation of the land happened there in the recent past. For example, around the ruined city of Tiahuanaco there are broad areas that must once have been cultivated in rice, but rice cannot grow at the altitude where the paddies are found. In addition, the city had quays, but it is now miles from the shore of Lake Titicaca and many feet above it.

It is also true that the largest earthquake to occur in the past twenty years took place in Bolivia. Measuring 8.3 on the Richter scale, the June 9, 1994, quake did no surface damage because it took place a mind-boggling six hundred miles beneath the surface.

The reason that this is so strange to scientists is that the rocks at that depth are supposed to flow. There shouldn't be anything that can break suddenly, which is what causes quakes.

Closer to the surface, a process called transformational faulting might explain the occasional quake that takes place in flowing rock as densities change. This does not explain how a quake could take place at a depth of six hundred miles, however. (It is also not explained by a possible crystalline core, either, which would be far deeper.)

Another thing about the Bolivian quake that was strange was the way it was felt at the surface. The highest intensities took place above the epicenter and at the edges of the quake zone in places like Canada and Tierra del Fuego. This bizarre pattern suggests that the core of the planet vibrated very much like a crystal.

If the core can be made to vibrate in ways that we do not yet understand, then it is conceivable that parts of the lithosphere could be shaken loose at times, with results that would range from the highly disappointing (the sudden elevation of farms to altitudes above the tree line) to the deeply depressing (the sinking of inhabited places into the sea).

Many other things that happened on that brief journey through time figured in my subsequent writings. For example, the idea that it could be possible to predict earthly weather by the use of solar probes wasn't even conjecture when *Nature's End* was written with its "solar probe" weather-predicting concept. At nine, however, I had seen the inset box on the television that clearly showed this being done.

In 1994 NASA announced Solar Probe, a joint project with the Russians designed to send a probe into the solar atmosphere to study it and begin to better understand the heliosphere (the sphere of influence of the sun).

Nature's End also predicted the droughts and the floods that have struck the Midwest, the commonplace use of encryption in computer transmissions, and genetic engineering. I do not recall any of these things from my early visions, however, at least not now.

One of the things that reviewers of *Transformation* were particularly derisive about was the prediction that the poles might melt, because this was based in part on predictions derived from the Marian visions that took place at Fatima. In the book, I pointed out that the *New York Times* had described 1987 as "a year of extraordinary glacial breakup." This process has continued and worsened. On April 29, 1995, *Science News* stated, "The floating Larsen Ice Shelf lost three major pieces earlier this year," giving off an iceberg the size of Rhode Island.

But the matter of the ice appears to be far more serious even than this would suggest. It was reported by Reuters on March 23 that Antarctica's continental ice shelf itself has begun to break up. Dr. Rodolfo del Valle, a prominent Argentine glaciologist and student of the Antarctic ice, said the first thing he did when he saw the tremendous forty-mile-long crack that now runs through the Larsen Ice Shelf was cry. Del Valle considers this an even more worrying sign than the giant icebergs that have broken off. The massive crack in the shelf exposed areas of the sea that have been under the ice for the past twenty thousand years. Del Valle said, "It was spectacular, because what once was a platform of ice forty miles wide had been broken into pieces that looked like bits of polystyrene foam . . . smashed by a child."

Scientists claim that even the partial melting of the ice could have catastrophic consequences, causing massive rises in sea levels.

One of the still-detached memories I have from my childhood involves ice coming down the sides of a mountain called Ben Bulben in the British Isles. In this recollection, I see England involved in a horrific catastrophe, a devastating change of climate that turns it into a deep freeze.

It is interesting that the suddenness of this change has recently been corroborated by new scientific insights about climate change. Researchers from the Woods Hole Oceanographic Institution, in examining ice core samples, have discovered that temperature changes of seven degrees Celsius may take place over just a few decades. "Our results suggest that the present climate system could be very delicately poised," according to researcher Scott Lehman, as quoted by Ross Gelbspan in the December 1995 Harper's.

What happened in the past was that the North Atlantic was warmed by fresh water coming in from increased rainfall and glacial melt, which changed the direction of warming ocean currents from northeasterly to due east.

According to the *New Scientist* of November 11, 1995, "relatively small increases in the amount of freshwater entering the North Atlantic could cool Western Europe by several degrees Celsius." According to oceanographer Stefan Rahmstorf, the weather will change radically if the fresh water flowing into the North Atlantic increases by 25 percent. Great Britain would become like Greenland over the course of a few years. If that happened, the ice would certainly flow down Ben Bulben once again.

The Texas pasture and farms I looked out on in my childhood future vision were profoundly distressed, as they would be if some sort of extreme change in weather had taken place. A change in average temperature and rainfall would be one of the things that could have caused such a disaster. Another would be a decrease in the thickness of the ozone layer. The strangely fierce sky I saw might be a clue to that. According to World Meteorological Organization Specialist Rumen Bojkov, the ozone depletion over the Antarctic "was unprecedented" in 1995, a time when disturbance of the Antarctic ice was also breaking records. Meanwhile, the ozone shield over the northern hemisphere has been thinning ominously for years, as evidenced by an 800-plus percent increase in the serious skin cancer melanoma between 1985 and 1995.

I am not a trained prophet. In our world, there is

no such thing. But my life in the secret school suggests strongly to me that human beings can sometimes see the future.

Like the other abilities explored in this book, there is no reason that the knack of prophesying need be confined to just a few people. As I have said before, one of my main points is that the states I describe and the benefits to be derived from entering them are available to anybody. It doesn't take special powers to do these things, but only the knowledge that one can. In that sense, being a visionary is as accessible as being a firewalker. Anybody who can get themselves into the right mental state—and that means almost everybody—can do this and live in the midst of this knowledge. Not only that, it has been my experience that the more one's compassion grows—the more open to life and grace one becomes—the richer the visions. The doors of the secret school open to the meek and the joyous.

But what is joyful about the world I saw on that TV? It appeared to be in an advanced state of catastrophe. It cannot be pleasant to live in such a place. Joy, however, is not happiness. Happiness we get from our surroundings. Joy comes from within. Perhaps the distinction can be made clear by saying that we left the joy of Eden in search of happiness. It may be that our greatest labor will be to find the joy that draws us together and makes us strong during a time when the forces of destruction are at their most powerful.

Aside from the obvious scenes of dislocation, such as the Asians on the road, there were many other smaller matters that add up to a clear picture of what may be a very real future world.

The planes I saw at the beginning of the sequence might have been anything from the F–15 on. They were not, in any case, very obviously advanced beyond what we have now. The TV could have been an ordinary color set or a high-definition TV.

The man I saw on the screen had a more strongly expressive personal style than television announcers have today. He was thin and I recall his paleness as seeming sickly to me. When he spoke, his voice sounded choppy. He seemed to talk very fast, and the images shot past at what seemed, in 1954, like an almost impossible speed.

CNN has almost reached that pace. In another ten or fifteen years, the five-to-ten-second "bite" will probably be commonplace in TV narration.

There was, on the face of the future Whitley, a complicated expression, reflecting, I would think, a sort of self-awareness that is very different from what I possess now. I am just beginning to understand life on the larger time scale, but I think that the Whitley of the future is quite familiar with meeting other versions of himself. I also think that he is somewhat like the people in the colliding galaxies might be, that he can perhaps count the days to the end of time.

We were one, the old Whitley and the boy, and as I write this, I feel that I am in concert with both. In a sense, this inner coming together is another meaning of communion, and why I said in my book of that name, "The human mind winks back from the dark."

Secret No More

"'Twas grace that taught my heart to fear
And grace my fear relieved . . ."

A New Lesson

IN THE SMALL HOURS OF THE MORNING OF NOVEMBER 12, 1995, I made another journey into time. It involved the first visitor encounter I have had here in San Antonio since returning for good.

I had been trying to make another such journey, to see if I could induce the physical state necessary on my own. What I wanted to do was meet my childhood self from my adult standpoint. The child had encountered the adult, so why not the other way around? Of course, if I do it at some point in the future, then I must already have the memory of it from childhood.

In point of fact, there is such a memory.

There was an incident in the spring of 1959 when I was sitting in my eighth-grade classroom and saw, hanging in the air above the blackboard, the head and torso of a man who appeared to be watching me. What startled me so much at the time was that I got the idea that he was me. I told the image, in my mind, that I would never, ever forget the moment as long as I lived.

Remembering it now, I tried to get the electric wave of ecstasy to pass through my body. I was trying to go back and become the man I had seen there, but that wasn't what happened, not at all.

As I meditated, I became homesick for my own childhood, hardly a state calculated to induce joy. When it had ended in August of 1954, I missed the secret school terribly, but when it ended for good in the summer of 1957, the loss was agonizing. It shattered my whole sense of self.

Without understanding its full implications, I described that moment in *Communion*. During a hypnosis session exploring the events of December 26, 1985, I suddenly flashed back to a similar incident that took place in 1957. This moment of hypnosis was the first hint that I'd even had any childhood encounters.

I was with the visitors and my father was present. I was watching a thin, willowy being with huge black eyes moving among long lines of American soldiers. All were on cots, all out cold. My father seemed scared. So I said to him, "Daddy, it's all right." When he replied, "No, Whitty, it's not all right," his fear just seemed to pour into me like a freezing torrent. I suddenly realized that the creature before us was the nun who had been my secret friend, and that she was really a monster. This was the beginning of the fear that ruled my life until the writing of *Communion* initiated the healing process.

After the summer of 1957, I never returned to the secret school, not until the rediscovery of the site in

1995. This discovery was also the discovery of my true childhood, of the boy that I was.

Rather than miss him, I decided that what I had to do was to surrender to my memory of him, to let him enter my life. He is a good guide for a dry old man: he brings torrents of joy, a shimmering sense of wonder, and a far more supple approach to the stresses of the unknown. He also brought me the journey that I was looking for—as usual, after I had given up on myself.

It began at about 4:15 in the morning, when I woke up with a fierce allergic reaction. I was sneezing uncontrollably, my nose was stuffed, my throat burned. Even though neither I nor my wife smoke, the bedroom reeked of tobacco, a fact that we both noticed. More than one witness has associated this smell with the coming of the visitors.

I went into the bathroom and used a nasal spray, but the sneezing continued. I took an antihistamine. By this time my eyes were swelling closed. To avoid further disturbing my wife, I moved to the second bedroom. I was lying on my side suffering when I glimpsed three figures come into the room.

This sort of thing has happened to me dozens of times. In the past, I often reacted by lashing out. My fear has dropped too far for that now, and so I became very still, not wanting them to disappear on me. I kept my eyes half-opened, watching as they approached with great caution. In my mind, I greeted them. Then, in order to open myself to them, I placed my attention on my body and quit thinking.

There was a series of loud noises inside my head. I have heard them before and described them to doctors, but so far they have no medical explanation. They are in the sonic mid-range, sounding at once mechanical and alive. Each time one occurred, I sensed that I had gone into a more altered state. There came to me the same loneliness that I'd felt back in 1983 when I seemed to go back in time at the corner of Houston and La Guardia in Manhattan.

Then I realized that the apartment had changed dramatically. I was no longer in bed, but lying on the floor. Things were scuttling under and over me. I jumped up, brushing myself off. Was this a recurrence of the dream of the insects that had troubled my childhood?

I looked around and saw that it was this same bedroom where I am sitting and writing right now, but it was empty. There were watermarks on the ceiling, and the window was broken. There were bugs racing around on the watermarked areas, apparently attracted by the small amount of damp. Big roaches were dashing about on the floor.

I rushed into the other bedroom looking for Anne, but it was empty, too. The bugs were everywhere, scurrying on the walls, packing themselves into places where water dripped.

I hurried off, heading for the living room. It was a complete wreck. There was no furniture at all, the windows were hollow frames, and the front door was entirely gone.

I was not in a panic, except that the bugs made the place extremely unpleasant to be in. I thought, You're either dreaming or it's worked and you've gone forward in time. I took stock of myself. I was wearing pajamas, I was barefoot. I felt physically whole, but I had finally acquired that familiar tingling that I associated with the old state of joy that I entered during sessions at the secret school.

Breathing deeply, I tried to stay calm. Now that I was no longer involved in the fear, I was feeling the true emotion of an experience like this, which is great ecstasy.

Sensing my body, I tried to stay in balance, to not let my mind go racing off into all the things I wanted to do. I wanted to find out if the visitors were out in the open, to see a car of this time, to talk to people, to discover the fears and hopes of the place. I wanted just a little glimpse of the stock market tables in a newspaper.

If I let my mind race, I knew that I would go right back where I came from. The state I was in is not automatic. It has to be maintained in a subtle, indirect way. Nothing can be forced.

I took my attention down to my solar plexus, then spread it through my whole body. I tried to let my mind just go blank. The effect was extraordinary. The tingling became a powerful inner throbbing. I felt like I was going to explode with life. My mind began flashing with images, my body seemed capable of going right through walls.

I went to the door, went out into the foyer, and faced the street. There was debris all over the place, and my feet were bare. I stooped down and picked up some shards of glass. Were they real? They felt real . . . but not like glass I might have picked up in an ordinary situation. I cannot articulate the difference, though, except to assert that, no matter how physically real all this seemed, it also bore some reference to dream. I would argue just as vehemently that it was no conventional dream and that we have not even begun to understand this state.

In this state, the universe has an immediacy that is amazing. It's as if everything that exists is right at hand. I could have walked on the moon or on Mars, gone to another inhabited planet, made a grand tour of the galaxy, entered a parallel dimension—anything. I could have gone anywhere just by inwardly turning myself in that direction. The presence of God was startlingly vivid—God was right there, in me, around me, everywhere and in all time. There was a sense of personality, of somebody who bubbled over with good humor, but who also addressed me with a stern sort of graciousness that was utterly sublime to feel. But God is a person—comprehensible as a person. A lovely, lovely soul and a dear friend, who is amused at the idea of human creatures starting to jump around in hyperspace—which reminded me of where I was and the fact that I had work to do here.

The first order of business was obviously to take stock of my surroundings. I looked across the street and saw that the older apartment complex that stands there now was gone. It hadn't been replaced, but rather destroyed. There was nothing there but grass and weeds. This shocked me, and I went out into the middle of the street. In nothing but pajamas, I felt vulnerable. But it was important to me to verify this experience. I had the glass, and now I wanted to see if I could get something else. There was plenty of trash around, so maybe I could find something with a date on it.

What I saw next, though, was a man. He was moving

along about fifty yards away. He was young, perhaps thirty, and wearing dark blue jeans and a white open shirt. I called to him, "Excuse me." I called again, "Sir?"

He stopped and looked toward me. His eyes seemed dark and hollow.

"Do you know what day this is?"

He said, suspicion in his voice, "Thursday."

My heart gave a lurch. It had been Saturday—or rather, the early hours of Sunday morning. It was *not* Thursday. I said, "I mean the date."

He said, "The seventeenth."

I went closer to him. "What year?"

He started backing away.

"Please! The year!"

He turned and began to run, but I think he said something. I think he said "thirty-six." It is just possible that it was "twenty-six," but I don't believe so. It certainly wasn't sixteen or oh-six.

He loped away toward a wooded area. These woods are there in the present, just beyond the complex that had disappeared.

I was trying hard not to get too excited. I felt as if I were on a tightrope. This all seemed real, I must say. The sense of dream was slipping away. I wanted to see more of the city. I looked down toward the shopping strip that, in 1995, is just below the apartment complex. Flat roofs told me that it was still there. I could see beyond it, but trees concealed too much for me to tell if any houses were standing in the neighborhood across from it. However far in the future this was, I don't know, but the trees were not dead as they had been in the time I entered when I was nine. That would seem to mean that this was a closer time, but later events suggested otherwise.

I looked back at my own condominium. It was very obvious from this vantage point that the place was abandoned. I wanted to find a newspaper, to see some cars, to talk more fully with somebody, just have thirty uninterrupted seconds with another person.

No sooner had I felt this wish than something greater than I was seemed to swoop down and take over. It felt as if I were flying about three inches above the ground, moving so fast that the world blurred. Then I found that I was in the neighborhood where I had grown up, which is only a mile or so from the condo.

I was standing on a familiar street corner, looking toward a large stone house that I have known since I was a boy, although I have never been inside it. There were two people in the front yard. They appeared to be collecting pecans, which would have put the event in the fall. So it was the seventeenth of October, November, or December in a future near enough for people to still do things like harvest their pecan trees.

I was watching the old woman bend when I realized that she was strikingly familiar to me. She was Anne, my wife . . . my very much older wife. I was deeply moved to see her across the gulf of the years. I called her name—but she did not stop, she did not seem to hear me.

The man with her heard me, though. He paused, then looked over his shoulder. His eyes were merry, almost as if he perceived the whole incident as a sort of practical joke. I knew that I was once again meeting my future self. I started across the street. He seemed almost to roll his eyes. I could see that he was laughing, and it annoyed the hell out of me. But when I tried to go closer, he reached down and got what looked like a piece of brick and tossed it at me.

He said something, and it was as if his words became my thought. The thought-form was, "This is one of many parallels. Put that in the book."

His voice was *so old*. It was not the same as the meeting when I was nine. I saw the devastations of age in detail this time. There was nothing anonymous or distant about this old man. He had sunken jowls, he was squat like my father had been in old age, his touch of hair was white and wispy, he moved as if he were made of glass.

The next thing I knew, I had returned to the condo, but it was still the ruined, abandoned version. I went into the second bedroom. The allergies returned, and I sneezed my way back down the halls of time to the present day. I understood why the Romans called— or call—their time-target the Temple of the Present Day: it was really as if I aimed myself into the moment that represented my present.

I was back on the bed. I sat up. Then I saw one of the visitors in the doorway. This individual was wearing a black cloak, the face was as still as a mask, the featureless eyes staring straight at me. I was not afraid of those eyes. To the contrary, I found that this terrible face—incredibly—is one that I have come to love.

I looked into that sculptured countenance, into those black and implacable eyes, but was not whipped by their power. What looked back at me this time was my own growing strength.

I stared at the visitor to make sure that my eyes were not playing a trick on me in the dark. The individual certainly appeared to be physically real, but there was no sense that it was alive. Its effect on me was contradictory—a machine, but a conscious one.

A terrific tiredness overcame me, and I curled up in bed. I sensed movement, tried to lift my head, then felt a hand on my cheek. Then I slept. I dreamed of the ruined condo, and this time it seemed remarkably filthy, the insects possibly even diseased. But the dream thankfully drifted away and I sank into blank, exhausted unconsciousness. When I woke up it was already nine-thirty. I heard a choir singing; it sounded like a high mass from long ago. Then a man began speaking and I realized that it was the radio in the next room.

I was shocked fully awake when it became clear that I could not understand a word that was being said. I sat up, listened. I couldn't understand English, not a word. In that moment, I felt as if I had gone a very long way this time. I had gone deep down some of nature's most lost byways.

Then Anne said good morning, and the sleepy familiarity of her voice brought a few words of English back. When the music started again I found that I could understand the Latin of the *Gloria* quite well. A few minutes later, the announcer came back, and I began to recapture my English.

We were planning to go to church with Ed Conroy and his family, but I could not find familiar streets. It was as if my memory had simply been erased. As Anne does not know the local streets well, we got hopelessly lost. Then I found that I could not make sense of the map.

Finally, we gave up on church and found a restaurant for breakfast. As we ate, I told Anne of my experience. I didn't have anything to show for it, not even the glass shard, but I did have something in my mind, something very new.

I have been working with this now for weeks, and the best way to describe it would be to say that I have come back with a possible memory from the future. First, from all the trips I have taken there, it looks like it will be a pretty worn-down place. The neighborhood I live in now in San Antonio has really taken some knocks. A lot of the housing is gone, the rest is in ruins, but the neighborhood nearby where I grew up appears to be intact.

Anne and I were still alive in that future. That seems rather fantastic, because in 2036 we will both be over ninety and we're hardly in perfect health now. The idea of living that long is shocking. Because we were so old and wrinkled, I didn't really recognize us; I just knew who it was.

Why were we out in that yard picking pecans? Could we have been hungry and stealing them? I don't know, and I don't think that it makes much sense to try and find out. It isn't the details of my own future that are important to me, it's the overall significance of the memories that I want to understand.

They are a rushing mass of obscure images, punctuated by things that are very clear. And one of those things disturbs me greatly. As a matter of fact, it is the most disturbing thing that I have seen in a whole lifetime of visions, and I want its importance to be acknowledged. I have been scorned and derided for years, but time has proved an awful lot of my visionary output to be authentic. I think that the country would be foolish to ignore this.

What apparently happened during my visit to the future was that I acquired access to some of the memories that I will have then, and they were not very pleasant ones. What I found was that, in this particular future, Washington, D.C., is in ruins. However, that isn't the center of the memory. The center of the memory is that it was suddenly and completely destroyed by an atomic bomb, and nobody knows who detonated it.

At the time of this vision, the United States is not a republic. In fact, it's in chaos. There are many things being done by companies that are now done by government. There is a congress, but not all states send representatives. The military is somewhat intact, and forms a shadowy sort of government. It is maintained by funds from the states, and there is a huge issue brewing about whether or not these contributions should be voluntary. I have the sense that there is a very brutal, shrill group of religious leaders—or people who so call themselves—who have made repressive laws that they want enforced.

When I realized that this was one of the memories borne in the mind of my future self, I initially thought that the destruction of the current government wouldn't be entirely bad. But it is not good. It doesn't turn out well. It's a human catastrophe on a massive scale, because it is too sudden and the shock leaves America dreadfully weakened and our whole world less free. It comes about because a number of different factors combine to make it happen. It is not done by governments, but rather happens because of their weakness and inability to police their own people.

A nuclear warhead is smuggled into Iran, thence shipped to the United States, where it is eventually detonated on the top floor of a building in Washington. I had the impression that the smuggling was done by elements of the former KGB and the Iranian secret police, who were not working for their countries, and that they were aided by a number of different religious and political groups both in the United States and outside it, groups that are even now deeply involved in our military leadership, intelligence community, and federal law enforcement agencies.

The conspiracy is extensive, and it appears to me now that it is already under way. It succeeds, essentially, because American intelligence is being blinded to it right now by a combination of bad planning and the presence of religious zealots within the community who support the idea and who are preventing information from being properly assessed.

Right now, we have two lines of defense against such an attack. The first is a covert intelligence system that is hopelessly outmoded, the second a detection system called Project HAARP that is full of problems, needs a great deal more testing, and may not even be what it is claimed to be, a system of detecting the presence of nuclear materials anywhere on the planet.

At present, the people who gather intelligence for the United States mostly work out of embassies. Their eyes and ears are attuned to the leaderships of their host countries. These spies, along with the so-called governments that they watch, are part of the past. Nowadays, to understand the world you must understand its extremists, because technology has enormously magnified their power.

Whoever is doing this intends to bring the components of their bomb slowly into the Western world, an unholy ark. The United States is breathtakingly vulnerable, because so much power is concentrated in the seat of government. If Washington were to suddenly cease to exist at a time when the entire government was present there, that would be the effective end of this republic. Historical forces that we hardly even notice now would overtake us.

We would suddenly have no congress, no Supreme Court, no president. There would be no one to turn to, no one to reestablish the structures that keep us free. Suddenly, fifty individual governors would have extraordinary power, along with the highest-ranking military officers who survived. The people would be completely helpless and the constitution would be a memory.

I don't think that a dictatorship would occur, at least not at first. What I have in my mind as "memories" from that future time is a sense of chaos and a feeling of immense decline. I feel that my wife and I are practically beggars, old as we are. In our personal lives, we are deeply at peace, but our world is not at peace and the country that we all take for granted now is no more.

Although this is not part of my memory, it must be that the United States will default on its indebtedness so extensively that it will have, in effect, become bankrupt. This would cause an enormous decline in the money supply of the world, resulting in headlong deflation, the collapse of all of our dependent currencies, and a depression on a scale beyond human experience.

I cannot confirm that I walked in that future world. The glass that I picked up was gone when I returned. But that doesn't really matter, in the sense that the commitment needed to completely change this particular part of the future is not a large one.

I cannot offer a method of protecting Washington. Enough plutonium to make a city-destroying bomb can be fitted into a space the size of a six-pack of Coca-Cola. In an article in the January 1996 *Scientific American*, the threat of nuclear smuggling is described as a real one. It turns out that we don't even know how much plutonium has been produced in the world, let alone where it is, and numerous attempts to smuggle it across various borders have been detected. *Scientific American* suggests that "systematic multinational measures be taken as soon as possible to inhibit theft at the source," but then concludes that, because countries are so reluctant "to recognize the severity of the threat," "such an idea seems very far-fetched at the moment."

This is obviously extremely unfortunate.

However, there is another method of guarding against the threat that isn't far-fetched, requires no investment, and does not involve any international cooperation. It asks for no significant institutional changes, no new international control bodies. It doesn't even require government to openly acknowledge the validity of my suggestion.

All that needs to be done is that the governors of a majority of states, right now, enter into a general accord to appoint a new congress in the event that a catastrophe destroys the old. They already have the right to make such appointments in the event of death or resignation, so no new laws need to be passed. This congress would then use the existing protocols to appoint a new president and vice-president, affirm the national debt, and keep the republic going.

Our republic needs a lot of changes, but it does not need a shock like this. We and our children do not need to be exposed to this danger. I think that this prophecy represents an effort on the part of a level of the human mind that is just now coming into focus. We are learning to prophesy, and as we learn, we will become more able to alter our future, to amend it, to change its nature.

It is important to remember that a real prophecy is not necessarily an assertion that a given event will take place. In this case, the simple actions that I suggest will make the attack pointless, and perhaps that will mean that it doesn't happen.

After this last journey into time, life in the secret school ended for me, well and truly. I was left with the understanding that it is a child's innocence that gives him access to the soul's immense store of knowledge and that I must somehow regain this innocence to go on. As I turn away from the long years of denial and fear, I find myself understanding for the first time the true meaning of Christ's admonition: "Except ye be converted, and become as little children, ye shall not enter into the kingdom of heaven."

We can find the path back to our old home, to the kingdom beyond time. We can look into the eyes of the children and there find the way.

The Path to Joy

HOWEVER, IT ISN'T ENOUGH SIMPLY TO REGARD THE children. We have to become like them. We don't know how to do that, because we don't remember what we have lost.

The secret school tells us exactly what we have lost: it's joy. "Have joy," the visitors said. In other words, participate in the true power of creation. Leap on wings of joy into companionship with God and the universe.

Children are friends of God, but we adults tell ourselves that the horrible state of the world means that God has left us. It doesn't mean that at all. Our world has left God.

Joy is a matter of being free, but we don't know what freedom is. People always ask me why the visitors don't just land on the White House lawn? Why all the secrecy?

We cannot have a relationship with the visitors because we are not free, and we are not free because we are not free in time. This means that we can have no objective understanding of ourselves and cannot see on a large enough scale to fully express ourselves.

So the nine lessons involved the manipulation of time, because learning how to use time as a tool is the key to reaching higher consciousness and a real relationship with beings—or parts of ourselves—who are already super-conscious.

When we reach that state, the secrecy will end because we will end it. Until then, we will keep it in force because we need it. When is then? The instant that we *see*.

The lessons, because they involved those journeys into the darkness night after night, also led deep into the heart of self. I did not find a dragon or a savage there; on the contrary, what I found was the amazed child that I was and can be again. However, Christ said to "become *as* little children," not "become little children," and the distinction is incredibly important.

We need to learn how to square the circle—to regain childhood's capacity for joy while preserving the knowledge and wisdom that we have gained as adults. Perhaps another way to say it is that, in order to find joy, we must return to our origins—in effect, to abandon the tools and weapons of the adult and take up a new kind of inner trust. Just when it seems that nature is about to turn against us, we must learn to trust her as never before.

We must listen as a child does to the words in the wind and the whispering of the stream, but understand as an adult does the meaning of the weather and the state of the water. Such is joy, a state of surrender that *knows* . . . but is quiet.

What knowledge must we acquire? Was the secret school a series of visions and dreams, or was it a real school with a real teacher? Looking back over the course of my life and my memories, I wonder how I am possibly going to identify the degree to which I am dealing here with fact?

One of the most amazing things about the whole experience is that it has any factual basis at all. And yet it does. Certainly, the secret school was physically real. I saw its ruins. Mrs. Carter was very real. The other people whom Ed Conroy found who'd made nocturnal visits to the Olmos Basin are real. The circle of friends with whom I remember going to the secret school are all quite real.

But the memories! What happened to cause them? And why did so much scientific corroboration occur literally as I wrote the book? This is why so many of the supporting references are to discoveries being reported in 1994 and 1995. It reached a point of synchronicity that was simply incredible. What I do know is that finding these memories, and so also my boyhood, was a lovely and delightful experience.

Great demands are made on me to fit the experiences that I report into some pigeonhole or another. Alien contact. Something that has been termed "the imaginal." Hoax, lie, or, as one magazine put it, the "astonishingly vacuous." The whole argument seems useless to me, given present knowledge. Something or somebody is out there, and that's where the certainty ends.

And so that's where the joy begins. Our relationship to the unknown can be direct, personal, humble, free, and fun, or fear can corrupt it and make it horrible. I know, it happened to me. But the terror can be put aside. It's not even very important.

We are at a glorious moment of change, and the secret school tells us just exactly how far along we are: it predicts that the next age will bring an end to the very types of order and authority that are presently so much in question.

In government, we are certainly getting more and more dissatisfied. All over the world, democracies are replacing dictatorships. Americans are incredibly sick of their own secretive, lying, and inordinately expensive governing system. People are beginning to want government to be concerned only with essentials, no more. In that direction, obviously, lies greater personal freedom.

In religion, we are beginning to cease to care about the differences between faiths. We are beginning to see that God's grace is extraordinarily abundant in this world—that people must actually work harder to avoid it than to receive it. It isn't that all faiths are becoming one, but that they are all coming to seem as valid to each other as they probably always have been to God.

Philosophically, science is fracturing. Physics is beginning to invade the behavioral sciences with strange ideas, like the one that perception may structure reality. So who perceived the world before we existed? Before any life? Questions like these are entering science in a rational manner . . . and so freeing science from the bondage of its old materialistic ideology.

Genetic research is starting to reveal that genes contain a vast amount of behavioral information, much of it incredibly detailed. Our genes are telling us that this is indeed a stage and we are actors. But who built the theater? Who writes the dramas? And, above all, why?

Struggling with these questions is being part of the secret school, sharing its freedom . . . and so also, its joy. The secret school suggests that we are the authors of ourselves, engaged in some extraordinary effort that we are only just now beginning to see with our ordinary minds.

What we are beginning to glimpse of our deepest selves is startlingly free, breathtakingly pure, full of courage and happiness . . . and joy.

As we make the transition to Aquarius, we are throwing off all the old control mechanisms. We are reaching toward a new kind of mind, one that can walk the past, read the future, and use psychic power with knowledge and skill.

The old authorities have already tried and failed to use the extraordinary powers of the human mind in service of their continued control. In December of 1995 former CIA director John Gates admitted publicly that the CIA had utilized psychics in projects such as Star Light. As usual, the media immediately related this to the "paranormal" and laughed at it.

However, patents filed in the eighties by defense contractor E-Systems, Inc., would suggest that nothing paranormal was involved, and an understanding of this can empower anybody to realize that we all possess psychic potential of our own. If government agents can successfully read minds and remote view, so can anybody.

The process, it seems, rests on the fact that the very tiny electromagnetic field that is generated by the brain is available to outside influences. Previously, it could only be measured by contacts that touched the skull, as in an electroencephalogram. But recent advances in circuit sensitivity have made it possible to detect it from a distance. Some patents suggest that it can also be deranged or intruded upon with correctly tuned frequencies.

In the public sector, there is also some leading-edge research involving the detection of thought. In 1995 researchers at the University of Tottori in Japan began developing a device that was sensitive to the formation of the P-300 brain wave, which is produced when we focus on an idea. With this, they hope to enable totally paralyzed patients to communicate by simple signals based only on thought.

Knowledge of how brain waves function and how to manipulate them has been held secret from the public. It is the true basis of the psychic programs undertaken by the government. The explanation for the extraordinary abilities that the mind sometimes exhibits, that media generally dismiss as "the paranormal," probably lies in quantum physics. Electrons inside the brain obey the laws of classical, or Newtonian, physics. However, this is not true of the ones in the micron-deep electrical field that surrounds it. In fact, they are in what is called a state of superposition: they are nonlocal, or undefined as to their structure and position. This means, essentially, that they can be anywhere and—conceivably—in any time.

There have been a few scientific papers published in public journals that discuss psychic phenomena in the context of quantum-physical principles. One of them, "Does Psi Exist? Replicable Evidence for an Anomalous Process of Information Transfer" by Darryl J. Bem and Charles Honorton (*The Psychological Bulletin*, Vol. 115, No. 1, 1994), gives an overview of the creditable research that has been done and concludes that psychic phenomena not only exist, but that quantum physics may well explain the situation in just the way I have proposed: "Bell's theorem states that any model of reality that is compatible with quantum mechanisms must be nonlocal: It must allow for the possibility that the results of observations at two arbitrarily distant locations can be correlated in ways that are incompatible with any physically permissible causal mechanism." The freedom that comes from understanding that things like psychic power are potentially part of physical reality has its own delicious joy connected with it.

How will we save ourselves from institutions that are now so outmoded that their confused and increasingly human-hostile activities actually threaten our future by both concealing an empowering discovery like this and seeking to use it in the service of secret mind-control experiments such as those suggested by E-Systems' patents? The future holds many ominous possibilities, certainly, but ordinary people are also competent and powerful. We have a good chance of throwing off the evil that binds us down.

As we find true knowledge, it brings with it a new spirit, open and free. With it comes the discovery that the old technological society is outmoded. Our minds will turn out to be the only technology that matters.

They will prove to be breathtakingly capable in ways now hardly dreamed of.

Another type of freedom will be revealed—that we need neither wealth nor the smile of fortune to have real power. We need only ourselves, as we are. Among the very oldest of our ideas are the concept of the soul and the notion that human consciousness may aspire to and reach a higher state. Both of these are incredibly ancient ideas, and they appear in the very first writings of our oldest civilizations.

The Egyptian god Osiris was the first hero to die and be reborn as a deity. The deification of Osiris established the idea that rulers could become gods. This was the basis of state power in many ancient cultures, including the Egyptian and the Roman. This continued into modern times in Japan, where until just recently the emperor was considered a living god. It was Christ who brought the immensely potent idea that resurrection was available to every human being, that all human beings bear within them the kingdom of heaven and thus are candidates for eternal life.

As we express ourselves into the next age, we will come to the prime moment of this species, when mankind gains complete mastery over time and space and lifts his physical aspect into eternity, inducing the ascension of the whole species into a higher, freer, and richer level of being. What will this be like? How can it be that it could happen now? Does the lost civilization of the past have any message for us at this critical moment?

As we move into Aquarius, we do indeed see authority weakening in almost every human culture and institution. The new willingness to entertain notions like the presence of visitors and to largely reject the refusal of the old authorities to deal rationally with such matters signals a new eagerness to form opinions outside the traditional control mechanisms. As those mechanisms fade, the unknown uses their weakness to attempt to break through into the conscious world, and we find ourselves inundated with reports of UFOs, aliens, and all sorts of weird and wonderful things.

Ironically but predictably, faith is rising even as the old world disintegrates around us. As the old hierarchies are abandoned, what will be found beneath them is a direct and deeply real companionship with a higher being. God, in this sense, is about to enter the ordinary world, and the destiny of our souls as companions to our creator is to be enacted at last.

Here will be found the original source of joy, the true engine of the human future. By learning to look at the world in the much larger scale suggested by the secret school, we can make the huge leaps in self-understanding so essential to a joyous life.

There are certain simple ideas that have come out of the secret school that seem to me to be exceptionally freeing. One is the concept of the past being ice and the future water. Using it, we can see time in a different way. The present becomes a mechanism that we use to make choices, not some sort of mysterious force over which we have no control. The past is consequences, the future potentials. And so all journeys into the past offer a limited potential to change the present. All prophecy is inherently conjectural, no matter how exactly it may mirror probabilities.

If time travel is indeed possible, the closer we come to the prime moment of our species, which is the moment we begin to be able to move through time, the more clear it will be that all these strange manifestations from ghosts to aliens are really artifacts of our own vision—what we see of the part of conscious life that has escaped time.

The vague mythological beings of the past that have focused into the aliens of the present will soon become ourselves as we become the very time travelers whose shadows haunt all our history, including the present. Understand, none of this means that I don't think that aliens are present. Given that faster-than-light travel has made the objections of Drake's Equation obsolete, if aliens exist, they are either already here or will be as soon as they create the right sort of mechanism. So, in the unlikely event that we aren't already dealing with them, we'd better get used to the idea that they are going to show up on our doorstep unless we get to theirs first. But their presence is not the central issue here on Earth. We are the central issue, and the acquisition of new tools of mind that will help secure us a future is our primary task.

It could be that true journeys through time are what will at last reveal the mechanisms that drive the evolution of our world. An interesting thing that I have discovered is that there are apparently images of us that exist outside of time—time forms, if you will—whose shapes contain revelations about us that are beyond our normal intellectual vision. The largest of these that I have seen appears to span the entirety of consciousness, including both the distant past and the far future. I cannot point to a specific experience during which this vision emerged into my mind. As I worked on remembering the secret school, it slowly came into focus.

It is a view of the progress of man seen entirely from outside the time stream. It appears in my mind's eye as an enormous object hanging in a blue space. The space itself is conscious, ecstatically so. It is as if the blue space is the mind of God and the glowing object the idea of man.

It consists of a shining dark globe at one end and a bright, sun-like one at the other. Between them is a huge, spiraling stream that starts out dead, dark black and glows brighter and brighter until it explodes into the sun-like globe.

As I understand this vision, the dark globe is the past civilization that I have glimpsed, the spiraling fountain is mankind moving through the chaos we call history, and the bright globe is what we will shortly become. What is happening is that the dark, inwardly turned souls of the past are using the freedom of choice granted by history's anarchy to find their way into the light.

We have almost come to the end of this ages-long quest. The ones who still suffer negative polarity are clinging to the old institutions in the futile hope that history will continue and their chance to change will not be lost. They are the authoritarians who run our world, trying to control the rest of us and hold back change.

Fear will eventually fall from every heart, and every one of us, in the end, will see. Those now clinging to control will realize that their future depends not on tightening their grip, but loosening it. What will unfold is an era as fully informed as was the civilization of the deep past, but entirely open in its orientation, animated by joy rather than fear. Where the old civilization had to sacrifice freedom to preserve its power, this new world will possess true balance—full knowledge combined with maximum freedom.

The absolute blackness of the past symbolizes the rigidly authoritarian nature of the past civilization. Indeed, its customs have echoed forward all the way to the present, where they persist still in our governments, our ritual-encrusted religions, and our moral lives with their emphasis on sin. We pray for forgiveness all the time. But how often do we thank God for the chance to do marvelous and wonderful things? How often do we pray out of sheer joy at the fundamental excellence of mankind? Being a friend of God is, first and foremost, fun.

We are passing into a great change of species, and no matter how loudly the old authorities may proclaim that this is not so, it is going to happen. The appearance of the unidentified flying object, now on videotapes that are impossible for thoughtful people to dismiss, is, as Carl Jung originally speculated, testament to great change—and it doesn't matter who the visitors are or where they are from.

Our moment in time, when population reaches its limit and the world as we know it ends, is not about death at all. It is about ascending into a new kind of life. Such is the message of the secret school, secret no more.

FROM THE AUTHOR

I HAVE ASSEMBLED A SHORT LIST OF PROPHECIES AND predictions for the near future. I intend it to be used as a validating tool for my work, and trust that I have been able to be sufficiently exact for this to be possible.

- Our present system of government, made unstable by debt, public disaffection, and the vast chasm between its secret and public sectors, will change radically in the context of economic disruptions brought on by serious environmental difficulties of various kinds.
- Specifically, I see problems with a food supply disrupted by violent weather: great storms in some places, horrendous drought in others.
- I see huge clouds of smoke over a great city— Mexico City. Popocatépetl is erupting.
- In the United States, there will be a struggle for control, fierce but not very bloody. The power of the military/industrial complex will end, and with it official secrecy. What will take the place of the old system will be freedom in the form of a republic that is real.
- Despite all the chaos, science continues to move from success to success. We begin to understand our

deepest selves. As we unlock the meaning of our genes, we will discover that human beings and human lives are constructed in such extraordinary detail that the presence of a level of super-conscious planning prior to and hidden within our lives, as suggested by the secret school, must be seriously considered.

- Fusion is perfected as an energy source and we will want to mine the moon for fuel, but there will be an obstacle to this that will be overcome only through profound personal and social evolution.

- Antimatter will be successfully created, contained, and studied. It will offer us the ability to devise weapons of appalling destructive capacity and small size, but also the chance to use it for the greater good in mega-engineering projects that will need power on an undreamed-of scale. Given the explosive power of antimatter weapons, we will also become able to deploy a meaningful system of defense against asteroids and large comets. In understanding how to contain antimatter, we will also discover how to gain access to parallel universes and eventually to traverse the universe at speeds bordering on the instantaneous.

- A man presently working inside a classified program will reveal knowledge of how psychic power works. Many research programs now secret will become public, whereupon the work will proceed with explosive energy. Average people will gain access to their own enormous psychic abilities as they realize that we all possess them and can learn techniques to make them work. Effective methods of teaching them will come into general use.

- Memory and prophecy will be understood to be

tools of the hyperconscious level of mind, and people will begin to use them as such.

- Time will also come to be a tool, and travel in time will become practical. As mind frees itself from time and thus approaches singularity of consciousness, nations as we know them—directed by power politics, greed, and lies—will end. They will be replaced by the only valid form of government that has any meaning to the truly free: one that is founded in love and organized around compassion.

- We will meet people from other worlds, the barrier between the living and the dead will collapse, and it will become possible for the individual to store and process huge amounts of knowledge.

- We will throw off the bondage of assumptions that we are small, weak, and frail, and discover ourselves a rare and precious creation, immensely talented and bearing upon this tiny scrap of stone called Earth a powerful responsibility to survive, to grow, and to partake of all knowledge in full consciousness. As we do this, we will also find that others on the same quest reveal themselves to us, and we will join hands with them.

- As science becomes increasingly honest, open, and powerful, it will begin to detect the presence of deity in an incontrovertibly factual manner. At that point, a Niagara of joy will flood the world as the species consciously joins the companionship for which it was created.

On balance, looking at the future I am grateful that I have a child. I have a message for the young people of this world: that there has never been a better time to be alive, for the age of wonders is truly upon us. The miracles begin with you.

MAIL

Whitley Strieber
5928 Broadway
San Antonio, Texas, 78209

E-MAIL

Whitley@strieber.com

WEB SITE

http://www.strieber.com

AFTERWORD

ED CONROY

DURING A SIGNING PARTY FOR MY 1989 BOOK *REPORT on Communion* at the Twig Bookstore in San Antonio, long-time local attorney Lanette Glasscock came to me with an astonishing story.

Mrs. Glasscock, the mother of Whitley Strieber's closest boyhood friend, told me that, while driving through the Olmos Basin on her way to the Twig, she had seen three equally large, glowing balls of light flying through the sky in a triangular formation—headed, she said, in the direction of the bookstore.

Momentarily stunned, I didn't know how to reply save to give her my thanks, once again, for all her help with my quixotic research into the world of Strieber and the visitors.

This was not by any means the first report that I had received of extraordinary happenings associated with the Olmos Basin. As early as 1987, Strieber had begun to recount to me his childhood memories of nocturnal bike rides into the Basin, which adjoins the neighborhoods of Terrell Hills and Alamo Heights, where he grew up. It was there, he told me, that he met with friends his same age—and the beings whom he remembers calling the "Sisters of Mercy"—to receive visions and lessons that would only later come back to mind.

Soon after that time, several other people came into my acquaintance, each of whom were witnesses to sightings of unusual aerial phenomena or encounters with strange beings in the area of the Olmos Basin.

What was it about this area that seemed to generate these strange occurrences? Is the Olmos Basin a doorway to another dimension, or is it a place that people identify with their delusions about aliens and UFOs? What I have discovered is that the Olmos Basin is a place rich in folklore, surrounded by residents who have a strong sense of place. In terms of San Antonio's urban design, the Basin is itself something of an anomaly. Four hundred years ago, a massive earthquake caused an area of about eight square miles to subside about forty feet below the level of the surrounding hills.

On that land, just three miles north of downtown, now grows an ancient live oak forest cut in half by two mammoth works of man. On its north–south axis, the Olmos Basin is bisected by the serpentine concrete ribbon of U.S. Highway 281. From east to west, the Basin is divided by the massive Olmos Dam, which turns the Basin into a lake when heavy rains would otherwise flood the central business district.

From the point of view of the red-tailed hawks that circle above the oaks, the Basin is a wilderness area bordered by soccer and baseball fields, punctuated by the spire of the chapel of the motherhouse of the Sisters of Charity of the Incarnate Word. Just west of that spire lies the legendary Blue Hole, one of the main springs that gives birth to the San Antonio River. No doubt the hawks feel an affinity for the four-winged angels blowing trumpets that adorn each side of the base of the motherhouse chapel spire.

Many times as I drive past those angels, I wonder about the nature of the beings whom Strieber and other witnesses have described encountering in the Basin. One man, who prefers to remain anonymous, told me a story very much like Strieber's. As a boy living far from the Basin on San Antonio's predominantly Mexican-American West Side, he would often ride his bicycle halfway across town at night, driven by an inner urge to visit the Basin.

On one such occasion, he said, he walked his bicycle into the Basin near what was then Incarnate Word College (now the University of the Incarnate Word) and found himself entering what he described as a "dome of light." Inside that dome, he met a radiant old man who smiled at him and made him feel at home. My informant told me that at that moment he lost consciousness, only to come back to full awareness astride his bicycle on Zarzamora Street, miles away.

In *Report on Communion*, I wrote that the first such person to come into my acquaintance and allow me to use his name was a San Antonio native named Ron McAtee. He remembered, as a child in the 1950s, witnessing a strange craft hover low over a playground next to Cambridge Elementary School, about a mile from the Basin. His account of that experience is included as an appendix to *Report on Communion*.

That event, and others almost as strange in the same neighborhood, produced in McAtee a life long attempt to recall his experiences in greater depth. Part of that effort involved his acquisition of an aerial photograph of the Olmos Basin, and a fascination with a certain part of the Basin near the ruined mill that once supplied flour to the early Irish settlement of Avoca, which would play a remarkable role in my future researches.

In early 1988, McAtee took me to see the old mill and grotto in the area. The mill's ruins consist of a small structure that once held a waterwheel, on the path that Strieber also remembers using in his journeys to the secret school.

Once we had gotten oriented by locating the old mill, McAtee showed me a spot in the limestone cliffs along the trail where a large, concave depression—a natural grotto—had been eroded out of the rock through the action of a now dried-up spring. It was there where a good friend of his recalled encountering, when she was still a girl, an apparent alien being. When he subsequently introduced me to his friend, I found that she had a remarkable story to tell that further increased my sense that the Olmos Basin is a very strange place indeed.

When I first visited that site with McAtee, I had not yet had an opportunity to walk through the Basin with Whitley Strieber. When McAtee showed me the grotto and the mill, I remembered that Strieber had previously told me he recalled an old mill near the place where he met other children in his nocturnal circle.

About a year later, on a hot August day, I introduced

Whitley and Anne Strieber to Ron McAtee, and we all
went for a walk into that same area that held so much
significance for McAtee. Perhaps it was the heat combined with the ubiquitous menace of fire-ant hills that
discouraged us from spending much time back there,
but our foray into the Basin did not stimulate
Whitley's memory in any noticeable way. One of the
factors that was missing for him, he said, was a certain
large tree—which as a child he had dubbed a
"baobab" tree—along the side of the trail. As the
baobab is an African species, I did not see how one
could be growing in Texas.

Seven years later, in the fall of 1995, I joined
Whitley Strieber and a television news crew as we
went walking through the Basin one more time, this
time with the deliberate intention of finding the site of
the secret school. After showing them the quarry, the
mill, and the grotto, I was at a loss as to what more
there possibly might be in that area when suddenly I
saw Whitley take off up a hill leading to the cliffs, following a trail that slanted at a low angle through
heavy brush.

That step off the beaten path is what led Strieber
to make the discoveries he chronicles in *The Secret
School*. For me, what was quite remarkable about
the location of the ruined bench and the "baobab"
tree was the fact that they lay less than twenty yards
from the location of the grotto and the old mill—in
the very same area that, for years, I had suspected
held a larger significance.

What kind of significance? The information coming to me from various sources pointed to several
equally valid ways of beginning to think about the

Basin. Take the testimony of former Terrell Hills resident Charles Cockerell, for example, who manages telecommunications systems for a large international corporation based in San Antonio.

Back in 1990, he sent me an unsolicited letter in which he described an unusual aerial event over Terrell Hills and an apparent nighttime "visitation" that took place when he was growing up there in the fifties. At the time, Strieber lived just a few blocks away on Elizabeth Road.

> Are there any other people from the same time frame (1957–1960) and location (Terrell Hills) that have experienced some sort of related experiences? I ask because I have always had very strong urges to wander about Terrell Hills (I run there two to three times a week). I feel very happy when I am there and I feel sad every time I have to leave, and I was wondering if other folks might get the same feelings.

I called him and told him that I had indeed met other people besides Ron McAtee who had told me of childhood experiences in the Basin and its surrounding neighborhoods.

I had sought out the woman whom McAtee had described as encountering the being by the grotto, and found her house to be filled with marvelous art, including a wonderful painting of an owl and a wonderously made medieval lute. As a girl, she said, she had seen a strange, large circular craft hover over her home on Patterson Drive, on the edge of the Basin, and very near the location that Strieber used to enter it in those days on his nighttime journeys to the secret school. She confirmed, too, her experience with the being by the grotto, whom she remembered as a very tall man dressed in a white robe.

I also met a woman who for years has taught at San Antonio schools who described her son's childhood artwork from years when he spent much of his free time playing in the Basin, especially along its creek beds and in its caves. According to her, it was characterized by images of dome-headed beings with large black eyes, whom he called his alien friends. At the time, she said, she completely dismissed such stories as the product of his imagination, but now looks back at it all and wonders.

In a recent personal interview, Charles Cockerell and I discussed his experiences further, and he stated that he felt as though he were searching for a place that felt like a kind of spiritual "home," where something very important happened to him when much younger. He mentioned that he continues to run frequently through Terrell Hills, still with the sense of longing for that place.

He also recalled experiences startlingly similar to those described by Strieber in *The Secret School*. Here is an excerpt from Mr. Cockerell's letter, describing an apparent out-of-body experience from his late teenage years:

> It was nighttime, and I was lying in bed listening to the radio, when I entered that twilight state characterized by immobility and feelings of anxiety. The room was

dark, but I became aware of several (six to seven) robed and hooded figures standing around my bed. I also had the feeling that I was lifted out of my bed. Above my chest what I took to be a door or rectangle "appeared," with an opening about three-fourths of the way up. I was immediately aware of angry eyes viewing me through this opening. I had the distinct impression that I was being reviewed or judged. After some time I had the impression that I was being rejected!

Cockerell wrote that although the experience provoked an intense, immediate feeling of anxiety, he resolved to relax. As soon as he did so, he experienced "falling" back into his bed.

What I find remarkable about Charles Cockerell is not so much his long-standing interest in a spiritual "home" in Terrell Hills, but rather that, as an adult, he has continued to develop himself in ways that grow out of his earlier paranormal experiences. For example, he has twice visited the Monroe Institute to take instruction in exploring out-of-body experiences and deeper states of awareness, with his wife joining him as a student on the second occasion.

From those experiences, he has come to hypothesize that, at the level of the unconscious mind, there exist deep structures and energy currents that unite him with people from his early days in Terrell Hills, indeed with anyone anywhere with whom he would choose to communicate.

This deep sense of union is very similar to one of

the central messages of *The Secret School*: That we are bound to one another by deep connections that we scarcely even remember, let alone acknowledge.

Why would a particular area such as the Olmos Basin play such a powerful paranormal role in the lives of people living nearby? There is a large literature regarding Earth's subtle energies, particularly developed by English authors such as John Michel, Paul Devereux, Nigel Pennick, and Tom Graves, among others.

All of these authors have tried, in various ways, to make sense out of the stone circles, "old straight tracks," and other ancient features that characterize the landscape of the British Isles. While they have their disagreements with one another, they are united in hypothesizing that the ancient inhabitants of what is today Britain and Ireland (not to mention a good portion of the rest of western Europe and even parts of North America) knew how to detect "nodes of power" on the surface of the Earth where special and remarkable energy currents pass between Earth and sky.

Michel, in particular, is to be credited with advancing public knowledge of the idea that the ancients created a network of energy channels (called "ley lines" in England) through which vitalizing energy was distributed. The groups of standing stones that dot the landscapes of European countries may be understood, in Michel's worldview, as devices that among other purposes served to attune and direct those energies, much as acupuncture needles are believed to do the same for the human body.

Paul Devereux and Tom Graves have observed that

such places seem to have an unpredictable effect upon both human consciousness and the forces of nature. Such effects, they observe, may trigger aspects of the human unconscious that produce experiences which we interpret as encounters with UFOs or entities.

Nigel Pennick, for his part, reminds us that it was commonplace in the ancient world to believe that every place had its genius loci, or resident spirit, which was often associated with particularly strange trees or with springs.

North America does not yet have such a highly developed body of literature dealing with the subtler aspects of its own landscape, but it is not lacking in great earthworks and stone structures equivalent in stature to those of England. The great serpent mound in Ohio and the stones at Mystery Hill in Vermont are two ancient examples, not to mention the more contemporary wonder of Coral Castle near Coral Gables, Florida, built by one man in a manner that suggests the manipulation and understanding of anti-gravity forces.

There are no prominent standing stone circles in the Olmos Basin, and, at first sight, it seems no more than a little bit of the Texas Hill Country inside the San Antonio city limits. Appearances are deceiving, though, for if one looks closely, it contains features that lend themselves to geomantic interpretation.

The site where Strieber discovered the remnants of his secret school are located only a few hundred feet from the Blue Hole and just up the trail from precisely the kind of strange tree that ancient Britons would have identified with the spirit world.

So what conclusions do I draw from my years of listening to people's strange stories and tramping through the Basin?

Taken at a literalistic level of interpretation, Cockerell's experiences, taken together with Strieber's and McAtee's and those of my anonymous witnesses, present the possibility that they may all have been involved in the circles of children, just as Strieber claims. I have found no evidence, however, that would definitively link them all together as members of Strieber's original circle.

Alternatively, the stories I have researched present the possibility that somehow people living in the area of the Olmos Basin may find it easier to occasionally "see through" things to another level of reality. Perhaps the Basin itself is an area of geomagnetic anomaly that makes such sightings and encounters more possible.

Quite candidly, although I am not a psychiatrist or psychologist, I have eliminated to my own satisfaction a third possibility: that all of my witnesses are suffering from some kind of pathological delusion. Each person I have mentioned is a competent and normally functional member of society. My research into the life of Whitley Strieber has convinced me that he has told the truth about his extraordinary experiences to the best of his ability.

So, too, I have come to accept the sincerity of everyone whom I have mentioned here. One does not need to be "psychic" to determine when a person is telling you a tale made up out of whole cloth—many ordinary signs from body language to tone of voice to eye contact will give a person away.

Most reporters nowadays would take one of two tacks to reporting on extraordinary experiences of the sort I have just described: sensationalization or debunking. Having become convinced that another reality interpenetrates our own and is engaged in attempts at communication with us, I have no desire to do either thing with stories that have affected people as profoundly as those described here.

Like Charlie Cockerell, I have come to hypothesize that all of humanity is connected at a very deep level of mind where there exists structures and energies that permit communication of truths that go to the very core of our lives. That level of mind, moreover, is not separated from the Earth itself, but is, in fact, deeply connected with it in an energetic sense, especially at certain sites where the energy seems to be more freely available.

Is the Olmos Basin one such place? I have come to seriously entertain the possibility that it is. Born into a culture that looks at land solely as real estate to be developed, I admit that I hunger for a sacred landscape. But the stories of the witnesses will remain, even if the last oak in the Olmos Basin is bulldozed to make way for yet another athletic field.

WHITLEY STRIEBER is the author of many novels and works of nonfiction, including such legendary titles as *The Wolfen*, *The Hunger*, and *Communion*. He lives quietly in the country with his wife and their cats.